TOUGH-MINDED
MANAGEMENT

Joe D. Batten

TOUGH-MINDED MANAGEMENT

Third Edition

amacom

American Management Associations

*This book is available at a special
discount when ordered in bulk quantities.
For information, contact Special Sales Department,
American Management Associations, Publications Group,
135 West 50th Street, New York, NY 10020.*

Library of Congress Cataloging in Publication Data

Batten, Joe D.
  Tough-minded management.

  Includes bibliographical references and index.
  1. Industrial management. I. Title.
HD31.B3697 1978   658.4   78-15465
ISBN 0-8144-5477-1
ISBN 0-8144-7620-1

Third Edition

Printing Number

10 9 8 7 6 5 4 3 2 1

IF I place two pieces of material the same size, shape, and form on an anvil, and one is made of granite, the other of leather, and then hit each with a hammer, what will happen? The granite will shatter into pieces, precisely *because* it is hard. It is rigid, brittle, and weak. The leather is barely dented, precisely because it is *not* hard. It is flexible, malleable, elastic, supple—it is tough.

And this is the quality of *mind* we are talking about here.

THE AUTHOR

Preface

THIS is not a book on principles of management. Nor is it a treatment of management theory. It was written in response to literally thousands of questions and problems encountered both in my work as a manager and a consultant and in seminars throughout the world. I have sought to set forth in it all of the main ingredients needed by the manager of a total organization or major department to generate profits and growth effectively and to achieve other worthwhile objectives in an increasingly competitive world.

The broad spectrum of subject matter was prepared to provide the executive as well as the aspiring executive with perspective, philosophy, and tools. Thousands of top people have expressed a real impatience to present such material to their key personnel in order to achieve a climate compatible with the needs of a fluid and ever shifting world economy. For tough-minded management as discussed here is still at a premium. The sometimes pungent terminology is the language of operating business and is calculated to make some readers wriggle uncomfortably. Some of the thoughts advanced may be new to the reader and require an eager and questing mind to assimilate fully. Some of the changes called for certainly cannot be accomplished in a bland and comfortable way—but the requirements of modern management are seldom completely comfortable.

The book does not flow in the traditional way, since I have occasionally shifted gears from a department or total organization focus to an international focus. I have done this deliberately: we cannot normally control the variables of operating management in textbook fashion. In short, I fondly hope this book is different—but completely realistic. Only time will tell.

Acknowledgments are always inadequate in a work of this kind, and I owe a profound debt to many people. Three principal sources of inspiration and help must, however, stand out. First, the distilled experience and wisdom of many associates, which were indispensable. Second, the interest of our clients, many of whom have become warm personal friends. Finally, the varied and stimulating experiences made possible by AMA, which is making a truly significant contribution to management throughout the world.

J.D.B., 1969

The years since the original writing of this book in 1963 have spawned a mind-boggling myriad of happenings. Now, more than ever, the times—our global community—cry out above all for management and true leadership.

It is my deep belief that there is no problem facing humanity on this planet that cannot be solved by sufficiently excellent leadership and management.

More than at any other time in history we must commit to optimize the human condition through clearer vision, deeper wisdom, tenacious commitment, self-discipline, and ACTION.

J.D.B., 1978

Foreword

I N his foreword to the original edition of *Tough-Minded Management*, Harry Bullis depicted the challenges to the modern leader and manager in his all-important role as a bulwark of support for our free enterprise system against the onslaught of state socialism. On the effectiveness of his efforts, as Bullis stated, the future progress of humankind depends. There is no doubt that the role ahead for our executive leadership will be a difficult task, albeit one of increased challenge and diversity.

In this revised edition of *Tough-Minded Management* Mr. Batten provides new stimulation to strengthen insights into the opportunities confronting our future business leadership; such insights will enable a manager to effectively lead the individuals placed in his responsibility and the organizations given him to direct.

One must realize that the fundamental theme supporting all of Mr. Batten's writings is the need on the part of every individual to recognize within himself the importance of continuous self-improvement. This carries with it the recognition that an individual cannot expect his personality to influence change on others and on his environment unless he is able to change his own attitudes, objectives, and intentions. The presence of a "learner image" within each of us is central to the expectation of maximum progressive change within an organization. Potential progressive changes within the organization are depicted with excitement, challenge, and pragmatism. Such an approach, of course, is totally consistent with, and inherent in, Mr. Batten's new, extensively covered idea of "confronting your possibilities."

The "learner image" within a managerial personality allows him to motivate associates and subordinates with the "loving critic" influence expressed by Dr. John Turner (formerly of the Menninger Foundation and now a practicing psychiatrist in San Francisco)—an image identical to that of a good father. Such an image stands in sharp contrast to the uncritical lover or unloving critic, whose characteristics result in ineffective management styles. "Strengths management" and "the management of strengths" are expressions that appear often in the new edition of *Tough-Minded Management*. They are integral to the loving critic image of a leader.

One will recognize in Mr. Batten's new *Tough-Minded Management* important emphasis on the challenges, pitfalls, and promises of the future. It should become apparent that one of the essential qualities of the image of a leader, in addition to those of an effective manager, is an ability to project the excitement of what the future might be.

Mr. Batten's new, mind-stretching insights concerning management by objectives—"MBO—A Living System" will enable leadership to move beyond traditional concepts of Organization Development to a more organismic approach which Mr. Batten has chosen to call "organizational actualization."

Like many of Mr. Batten's previous publications, this edition of *Tough-Minded Management* is a landmark in the understanding of our human institutions and the motivational techniques useful to those who enable the institutions to function.

Donald Alstadt
President & Chief Executive Officer
The Lord Corporation
Erie, Pennsylvania

Contents

Foreword   *ix*

1   Management Today   **1**

The True Meaning of Vitality • The Search for Security • Concepts of Personal Dignity • Opportunity—Yesterday and Today • The Pursuit of Ease • The Need for Purpose • Leadership Must Be Positive • Know Yourself • Mistakes Within Reason • Imagination and Executive Isolation • Two Fundamental Truths • To What End?

2   The Motivational Climate   **13**

Some Do's and Don'ts • Top Management Lays the Keel • The Taut Ship

3   Performance Is All That Matters   **22**

Dangers of "Realism" • The Only Reason for a Salary • Making Things Happen • "Nice Guy" Management • The "Methods Improvement" Panacea • Return on Investment—Fact or Fallacy? • Court of Appeal

4   What Is Development?   **32**

The Structured Approach • What It Adds Up To • Opportunity to Stretch • Separating the Pros from the Amateurs • Growth Is Personal • The Elusive Essential

5 Plan for Accomplishment   41

Why Don't We Plan More? • To Get Participation and Cooperation • The Importance of Being Consistent • The Vacillating Vice President • Don't Listen to "Activity" • What Do We Do About It?

6 Organize for Results   49

What It Takes • Get Operational! • Wasted Talents • The "We" Feeling • Clear-Cut Assignments • The Delegating Executive • Accountability Is Common Sense • Profitability Accounting

7 Motivate Your People   60

Basic Needs and Personal Goals • Communication—Shared Meaning—Shared Understanding • The Role of the Individual Manager • The Common Denominator • Decisions Must Be Made! • When Emotion Is an Asset

8 Control and Insure Progress   73

Where Are We Going? • Blind Dedication Can Be Costly • More Paper • Some Kind of Feedback • To Measure Performance • Follow-up Can Make or Break You • Controls Must Pay for Themselves

9 Stressing Positives for Tough-Minded Results   83

The Real Challenge • The Little Person • Defense Mechanisms • Sarcasm—Expedient of the Weak • Cynicism—Corrosive Refuge • Fear Can Kill • Make Tension an Asset • Let Yourself Go

10 Action Words and Concepts   93

Overcoming Resistance to Change • Think Big but Speak Simply • Reports: Get to the Point • Memoranda—Why? • Effective Interviewing • How to Sell with Words • The Word Picture • He's a Smart Man, but . . .

11 Phonies Finish Last   102

Who's Fooling Whom? • The Price Is High • Why Dignity? • Build on Granite • The End of the Story

12 The Essential Lubricant   108

Face to Face • Committees and Candor • Counsel—Don't Advise • Rough Going for Politics • The Prevalence of Yes Men • Businesses Are Composed of People • Stimulating Constructive Innovation • The Only Way

13 Courage and Logic   118

New Styles in Bossism • More Pull than Push • The Course of Least Resistance • Don't Fetter Your Imagination • Problem Solving in the Motivational Climate • Becoming

14 Work, Warmth, and Wisdom   126

*Elementary Common Sense • Prescription for Longevity • Drudgery
Depends on Attitude • The "Clean Desk" Executive • The Martinet •
The Stuff of Management • A System of Values • Work Is Life •
Warmth and Empathy*

15 The Electronic Age: Problems and Blessings   137

*The Kaleidoscopic Decade • Automation—Servant or Master? • The
Objective View • The Operations Research Techniques • Mathematical Parameters • Organizational Impact*

16 The Free Enterprise Way   147

*Ideas That Build and Strengthen • The Sterility of Materialism • A
Better Job of Selling • Talk About Profit*

17 Management in the World Arena   155

*Multiple Obligations • Our Resurgent Allies • The Common Market •
The Disciplined Executive*

18 Above All, Integrity   161

*Free Enterprise for All • A Working Definition • Integrity Must Be
Pervasive • Growth of a Business Conscience • Why Integrity Is Natural • "The Young Sophisticate" • "The Old Smoothie" • Ramifications of Management Decisions • Community Impact*

19 Profile of a Tough-Minded Manager   171

As an Individual • As a Member of Society • As a Manager

20 The Challenge of the Future   177

*The New Person • Some Thoughts About the Future • Population •
Labor • Education • Mental Abilities • Longer Life • Genetic Engi-
neering • Medicine • Nuclear Energy • New Worlds to Conquer? •
Some New Tools*

**21 Tough-Minded MBO—A Living System of Human Dy-
namics**   196

*The Need for Significance • "Becoming" in Response to Expectations •
The Human Element and MBO*

22 The Fully Functioning Organization   209

OD or OA? • Considerations for the Future • The Peter What?

Index   219

1

Where do we go from here?

Management Today

Traditionally, an examination of management principles, processes, and practices has looked to the past for perspective. Current literature is replete with accounts of the development of scientific management: the contributions of Taylor, Gantt, the Gilbreths, Mayo, and others. Our concern here is with the present and the future.

A bitter indictment of much of modern business is found in William H. Whyte, Jr.'s *The Organization Man.* In contrast, let me say clearly that the succeeding chapters are not intended as any such indictment of business as a whole. I do discuss certain weaknesses in order to point up what is needed. And the first essential ingredient, it seems to me, is vitality. Innovation, creativity, tough-mindedness, and, in the final analysis, end results are not possible without it.

The True Meaning of Vitality

Sheer physical fitness and/or mental sophistication is not enough. These qualities are found in reasonable abundance in business today. A vital awareness of the basic purposes of life, and an awareness of the relationship between these purposes and productive work, are essential.

1

Are the multitudes of scurrying people with quick obsequious smiles, pliant platitudes, and trite truisms vital? Vitality implies durability and smacks of toughness on the face of it. But just ask typical young management people what their personal goals are. The answers will usually fall into a stereotyped pattern: "I want to feel secure, make a good living, send the kids to college, and take some nice vacations." Or, "I want to make the most money I can, own two cars, have a nice home, and belong to a good club." These quotations are taken out of their total context but are discouragingly descriptive of the main goals of many young executives and, all too often, older ones too. They are seldom aware of the over-all goals or objectives of their organizations, and to an even lesser extent are they able to identify with them.

This apathy, then, is a condition which is not solely a fault of the lower echelons. There are middle and top management people whose lives appear to lack direction, possibly because, for one reason or another, they have lost ambition and interest along the way. More serious, however, for the future of American business is the case of the younger executive. The old saw, "The shortest distance between two points is a straight line," was never more apt than here; plotting this shortest distance presupposes an appropriate goal. People simply cannot fulfill their potential if they lack worthwhile personal goals, and they cannot make the optimum contribution to the company's goals if they fail to know them and identify their own with them—and, consequently, fill their days with bustle and activity for the sake of a paycheck.

This activity and bustle should not be confused with vitality. The vital life is one in which the whole person is challenged. He or she must be called upon by tough-minded top management to *stretch*. He or she must experience a quickening reaction to the results required: results that cannot be realistically set until top management faces up to its primary obligation, which is to determine what the organization is committed to doing and then stretch all its people toward optimum use of their abilities in this direction. The motivational climate, which will be mentioned often (see Chapter 2), is calculated to provide tough-minded management with the philosophy and tools needed to unleash and utilize the vitality that is latent in most organizations.

The Search for Security

It is disturbing to note that the word "security" has become increasingly popular in almost inverse proportion to the increasingly reluctant use of the word "profit." We all know of people who have no occasion for financial worries of any kind. How many of these people appear to be really happy with their role in life and their image of themselves?

There are exceptions, of course, but the majority do not have a feeling of real security. Security is about 20 percent financial and 80 percent emotional. What, therefore, does it take to achieve emotional security? Basically, it takes a mature awareness of one's role in life, of which one's job normally is a major part, and a knowledge of what to do about it. Rudyard Kipling's "six honest serving men" have been cited so often by writers on management that I hesitate to introduce them here, but their usefulness in achieving emotional security is obvious:

> Know *what* you want and have.
> Know *where* you have been and where you want to go.
> Know *when* you want to go—have a timetable.
> Know *why* you want to go.
> Know *how* you will use your own resources and the talents of others.
> Know *who* will be involved.

The formula may appear absurdly simple, but it is estimated that, at most, 10 percent of the management people in our country today can readily show evidence of this kind of self-analysis and planning. Personal earnings is *not* the answer to today's search for security. Self-confidence, self-knowledge, and an awareness of what you stand for will do much to insure it.

Concepts of Personal Dignity

Much has been written in recent years about the need to make the individual employee feel important—feel needed, feel like something other than just a payroll number. What does tough-minded management call for in this area? Is it inconsistent with traditional human relations concepts as applied to the job?

Actually, it involves much more than the belief that employees are stimulated and motivated to greater productivity through "do-gooder" devices. The tough-minded administrator realizes that simply trying to make people feel good by means of service pins, name plates, mentions in the house organ, and other "devices" is not enough. Granted that all people have basic dignity, it follows that they must have a distinct feeling of both purpose and contribution.

It must be understood further that there is no reason for being on the payroll other than contribution to organization objectives through the accomplishment of departmental and individual objectives. These must be wedded and welded together in a manner that is meaningful to the individual; else his dignity will be impaired. It follows, also, that genuine recognition cannot be accorded an employee if you know and he knows that he is only "busy" and does not make any real contribution to departmental or company objectives.

Many of our faceless "organization men" have become pliant, conforming creatures because of their organization environment. In the absence of real performance yardsticks or criteria, it is often natural to arrive at the conclusion that the path to promotions and raises lies in the direction of ear banging, the collection of status symbols, acquiescent behavior, "sophisticated" parroting of accepted concepts, internal politics, and many other safe courses of action.

Is this personal dignity? The tough-minded executive knows otherwise.

Opportunity—Yesterday and Today

Opportunities for growth, contribution, and true success were never greater than they are today—from both the corporate and the individual viewpoint. New-product development is looked upon all too often as a panacea for sagging sales, seasonal fluctuations, dipping profits, and corporate politics. The mortality rate for newly conceived product ideas is approximately 98 percent, not so often because the basic idea was poor but rather because of poor planning, organization, coordination, motivation, and control of the research, development, production, and marketing efforts. Here, then, is a real focal point for top-level attention and one of the principal reasons for a book on tough-minded management.

What about the individual? What about the many senior and junior executives and non-executives who bewail the lack of personal opportunity in America today? The bald fact is that there are far more big jobs than there are big people. It behooves the little person to become a big person or quit griping. The motivational climate created by tough-minded management makes this kind of growth possible.

Today's executive must be broad-gauge, and this should constitute the finest sort of challenge to the individual emerging from the shop, or to the college graduate whose training has consisted largely of principles derived from various academic courses. To quote Lawrence A. Appley, former chairman of the American Management Associations: "Management is the development of people, not the direction of things." The full significance of this truth has not registered with many present and aspiring management personnel. The person who wishes to prepare for the broad-gauge top management position must realize that production, marketing, engineering, and financial problems are caused by people and can be solved by people. *Thus an enlightened, tough-minded approach to management requires a thorough knowledge of how to develop and motivate people. Without this, few can qualify for the big assignment.*

The Pursuit of Ease

The Syrian poet Kahlil Gibran has said: "Always you have been told that work is a curse and labor is a misfortune. But I say to you that when you work you fulfill a part of earth's furthest dream, assigned to you when that dream was born, and in keeping yourself in labor you are in truth loving life. And to live life through labor is to be intimate with life's inmost secret."

It is almost a truism that the busy, productive, outgoing mind is the happiest, yet this concept seems to be eluding the majority of contemporary Americans. Listen on a Monday morning to the tales of what happened over the weekend. Note the zest with which most people look forward to vacations. This is healthy and normal. It is not so healthy and normal, however, that so many dread—or pretend to dread—the return to work. Undoubtedly this is a reflection of the desire to conform (when we were youngsters, after all, we never dared say we "loved" school, we "hated" it), but what sort of thinking is it that views time spent on the job as time sacrificed till we can again enjoy ourselves?

It would not appear to be part of God's plan for people simply to tolerate their wage-earning chores. Many sprightly old people in their eighties and nineties have been interviewed and studied to determine the reason for their longevity. A common denominator in these findings is usually the fact that they enjoyed their work, worked hard, and gave freely of themselves.

Clearly, something vital is missing from the typical organizational environment. The will to create, to produce, to mold and build, and, above all, to *give* just isn't there. To repeat: This is abnormal, rather than normal. We have often heard employees say that they'd like their work, too, if they had a soft touch and a high salary like the company president. Yet research has shown that the average top executive *made* things happen to him instead of waiting for them to happen. He was not preoccupied with security. He reacted to the requirements and privileges of our free enterprise system with individuality, a generous expenditure of midnight oil, and tough-minded follow-through. This is the only way to get there—short of being born the boss's son or daughter—and it can, and should, be fun.

The realization that productive work is one of life's greatest pleasures is not just desirable—it is absolutely essential to the maintenance of our democratic free enterprise system. It is crucial to "get a lot done and have a lot of fun." You can't do much of one without the other.

The Need for Purpose

Life without productive work directed toward some purpose is meaningless, sterile, and messy. Take a look at some counterculture people—those vapid, vacuous, and crushed-looking creatures. The principal things they lack are purpose, insight, and self-discipline.

The two requirements are intertwined. Discipline is needed to look at yourself squarely and define a role, or purpose, in life. Further discipline is needed to face up to your management responsibilities and help your subordinates determine purposes and goals. Delinquent behavior is only one of the current symptoms of life without purpose—of reaction to pressures to conform. The alcoholic, the playboy, and the malcontent are reacting in other ways.

The story has often been told how Wernher von Braun, the great rocket scientist, once flunked a course in mathematics. At that time he had no particular objective but to finish school, but eventually he began to read about rockets and space, decided that this would be his field, and learned how necessary mathematics would be. He then proceeded to take all the mathematics he could in order to reach his target. In the end he discovered a real zest and pleasure in tackling the roughest problems.

It is imperative that we cease to regard work as a means to an end—a chore to be disposed of so we can enjoy ourselves. Productive, results-oriented work should be viewed in its proper perspective as an integrated, essential, and pleasant part of living. Time after time, people who have reached or are approaching retirement express keen regret at having wasted many productive years in dreams of ease and leisure. They realize belatedly that the opportunity to live richly and fully—to experience the pleasures that can come only with accomplishment—has passed them by.

Leadership Must Be Positive

Motivated people who *want* to work because they know *why* they are working are essential, then, to the successful business—as they are, indeed, to any successful effort. Job Methods Training (JMT), Job Relations Training (JRT), and Job Instruction Training (JIT) all had their inception years ago and served their purpose fully. These courses provided carefully worked out approaches to greater efficiency. They provided uniformity, order, and system. But they were successful primarily because they were taught within the framework of a greater purpose—to defend our country and protect our way of life.

For many years programs in leadership training have proliferated like rabbits. Most of them have not proceeded much beyond JRT, JMT, and JIT. By and large, they leave much to be desired. The manager or supervisor is scheduled for a training session by the boss—so he goes. He is pretty much told that "techniques," "procedures," and "methods" are good because they are good. These seldom are clearly related to company, departmental, and personal goals. Hence there is no stretching of the imagination, no pull, no real motivation, nothing for a person to sink his teeth into and walk out with recharged batteries. Is this what it takes to meet the world challenge? The positive leader/manager knows better.

Positive leadership need not be clothed in any complex terms or abstract concepts. Positive leadership, simply defined, means the kind of direction which assumes that the job can be done, the problem solved, and the negative attitudes overcome until proven otherwise.

What of these negative attitudes, particularly in the manager himself? Is there a place for the person who is adept at inserting so-called "realistic" considerations into every new idea or innovation that comes up? Many decisions are made in the name of realism when actually the determining factor is simply an unwillingness to face up to the sacrifices, the hard work and sweat that truly significant achievement requires. In many board rooms and conference rooms (and in first-line supervision) we have people who invariably argue that a thing can't be done. They are good, many times, at stating the problem or pointing out what's wrong. But, while problem-solving skill is sometimes at a premium, it does not take real imagination, real courage, or, in the final analysis, real ability simply to put one's finger on the spot that's causing the trouble.

The positive leader asks this question often: "All right, now that we know what the problem is, what do we *do* about it?" The positive leader must have confidence; he must believe fundamentally in himself; and this type of deep, sustaining confidence cannot be developed in the classroom or in the management development programs now so popular in many industries. Real courage and self-confidence, in depth, are acquired only by meeting a problem boldly and overcoming it.

The positive leader trusts himself. He knows, following adequate research, what has to be done and does it. He is impatient with people who want only to tell him what the problem is; who simply want to talk about what is wrong. He is sometimes considered almost abrupt and even abrasive in his insistence upon determining what the end results should be and what should, in fact, be done.

True self-confidence is necessarily a product of self-discipline. The person who cannot control his yearnings for leisure and the easy way will seldom feel pleased with what he sees when he examines himself.

Know Yourself

We often see top executives who work themselves into a state of turmoil, frustration, and confusion because their subordinates don't seem able to anticipate their every whim; and what was right yesterday is wrong today. Very often, these executives just don't understand themselves. They have not taken an objective and penetrating inventory of their own personal goals, desires, strengths, and weaknesses; and it is fundamental in attempting to motivate subordinates that superiors must at all times know what they, themselves, actually want.

Here is a real place for tough-minded thinking. The courage to look objectively at yourself, to recognize strengths as well as weaknesses, requires real effort. It's the kind of thing we are tempted to defer. After all, the boss is the boss, and if he is sometimes temperamental and his whims are somewhat irrational, isn't that one of the prerogatives of top executive assignment? Remember, however, a weakness is only the absence of a strength.

At this point it may be well to distinguish between autocratic behavior and tough-minded performance as advocated in this book. The fallacy that it is the strong, or tough, executive who fires a lot of people, who regularly administers tongue lashings and cutting rebukes, needs to be exploded as the myth it is. What kind of courage is required to call a defenseless subordinate in and dwell at length upon the individual's weaknesses? You have the superior position, the authority; the subordinate has no recourse but to take the abuse without talking back. At the other extreme, obviously, is the manager who cannot face up to the situation when disciplinary action is definitely required.

Although it is sometimes difficult, the most productive path to follow here is to "build on strengths, not focus on weaknesses." This means that you develop increasing proficiency in telling the subordinate what he is capable of and avoid dwelling at any length on what he has not done well. This may not sound tough-minded, but it requires more resourcefulness and skill to use this positive approach than simply to pull rank and elaborate on weaknesses. It has been proved many times that, almost automatically, those areas which have been weak will be taken care of.

In the same way, knowing yourself involves the ability to ferret out and focus on those strengths *you* have and to avoid the comfortable refuge of hiding behind your shortcomings. This may sound backwards. Isn't it true, you argue, that we see much egotistical and conceited behavior in top company executives? Perhaps it is; however, such behavior is seldom displayed by the man or woman who possesses a deep and basic belief in himself or herself. Evidences of conceit or cockiness usually are closely related to personal feelings of inadequacy. The tough-minded manager takes an honest look at both his own and his subordinates' attributes, maximizing the strengths so as to minimize and correct the weaknesses.

Mistakes Within Reason

What about the purported high incidence of ulcers, nervous breakdowns, and heart attacks among executives? The alarming statistics of several years ago have largely been disproved. The capable manager with a strong sense of direction, and with abundant courage, is now considered a good insurance risk.

The corrosive acid nibbling away at the vitals of the troubled executive is almost always some kind of fear. Fear of what? The fear of mistakes in judgment, with the resultant loss of position, job, and material advantages, is a prime offender. Indeed, to make a mistake has become a cardinal sin in many businesses, and this has resulted very directly in the diminution of vitally needed innovation and creativity.

The motivational climate encourages mistakes within reason. It recognizes that ambition and high productivity must result in a certain number of them. It recognizes that the only way to avoid mistakes completely is to do nothing. The Maytag Company, which is consistently regarded as one of the nation's best-run businesses, has laid down a basic managerial philosophy which allows for mistakes in a calculated invitation to innovation and improvement. The wings of the young eagle who never exercises them become ineffectual appendages; ultimately he fears even to attempt to fly.

Imagination and Executive Isolation

There is much current talk about structured interviews, structured group dynamics, structured management. Many executives have sought—and are seeking—a precise, quantitative administrative environment which functions with the inexorable precision of an automated system. This includes a place for everything and everything in its place; clean desk tops and a work day that consists solely of planning and control.

Management of this type does contain some desirable elements but seldom works out in actual practice. It is pretty sterile and antiseptic. The tough-minded manager realizes that a good amount of contact with subordinates is essential to coming to grips with the problems of the business. His imagination, his creativity, and even his daydreams lose much in the process of transmission through memoranda and reports. Imagination, literally, calls for seeing an image of what should be done and breathing action and life into the vaguely seen picture so that it becomes an understandable concept or project. A fertile, creative mind will become dulled without a good bit of day-to-day exposure to other people's experiences, achievements, and foibles.

It follows, therefore, that the tough-minded executive does not create from and administer solely by charts, statistics, memoranda, and reports. He receives the charged current of inspiration from "people" situations and faces up to the requirements of those situations. To retire into the inner sanctum of the executive suite and make decisions from this insulated position seldom appeals to him; he is more concerned with results than activity.

Two Fundamental Truths

In an effort to help the manager deal with people and get things done through them, the field of human relations practices and training has been pretty extensively cultivated in the past 20 years. The principal emphasis in some quarters was on developing relationships between superior and subordinate which made the subordinate feel he was understood and made the superior feel himself master of the technique of human manipulation. Recently, however, we have begun to come of age in the practice of human relations. The most capable managers are realizing that studying human reactions, habits, and performance is not a separate discipline or technique but, rather, an essential and integrated part of day-to-day management.

The manipulative approach largely overlooked two things which are basic to human nature and which are being asserted more and more:

1. People want a hand in determining the direction to be taken in their jobs or departments. They cannot be "led" by the supervisor who makes a meaningless habit of asking about the wife and kids or administering a pat on the back when the employee knows it was not genuinely earned.
2. People are basically happier when their work provides them with stretch, pull, and challenge. Most managers, surprising as it seems, do not expect enough from their people.

To What End?

Why should managers today expect more—of themselves and of their people? Why is the quality of business leadership more crucial than ever before?

Our abundant and opulent standard of living, our rights and privileges, are facing their most serious threat. How is this possible when, materially, we were never better off? Because, with cold calculation, the forces of collectivism are exploiting our most obvious weaknesses throughout the world:

1. The worship of leisure.
2. The deification of recreation and amusement.
3. The pursuit of financial security.
4. Fear of innovation unless it provides immediate returns in money or leisure.
5. The loss of hard-nosed individuality.
6. Refuge in mass thinking and collective movements; sheeplike behavior.
7. A tendency to talk rather than act.
8. Lack of awareness of our own history.
9. Failure to take a strong stand for individual beliefs.
10. A tendency to view the future with trepidation.
11. Spiritual exhaustion.

The great need is for *purpose* and *direction*—for vitality, guts, and a positive approach. The principles of democracy as embodied in free enterprise do not have to be explained or defended. They must simply be practiced within a framework of dedication, the giving of self, and hard work.

At this early juncture, let's understand clearly the meaning of "toughness" and of the "tough mind." Granite is *hard* and can be smashed by a hard blow. Leather is tough and can only be resiliently dented by a hard blow. Hardness is usually brittle, static, and weak. Toughness is supple, flexible, and durable.

2

Develop a clear and complete system of expectation in order to identify, evoke, and use the strengths of all resources in the organization—the most important of which is people.

The Motivational Climate

THE motivational climate is that atmosphere in which your people work hard and productively because they *want* to. Here are the ten essential steps in achieving it:

1. Lay out clear over-all company objectives and direct the strengths, energies, and aspirations of all the organization's people toward objectives or goals in harmony with them.
2. Select the best people for appropriate jobs. This means using suitable screening and hiring tools—including, if necessary, tests tailored to job requirements. The ability to screen and hire good people systematically for key positions is a talent pathetically lacking in many of our present management personnel.
3. Define job duties and performance requirements. Insure that every employee knows the *what, where, when, who, how,* and—above all— *why* of his job.
4. Establish accountability for results in key jobs throughout the organization and provide for the necessary feedback.
5. Regularly evaluate the worth of every department, job, and person in the company in terms of contribution to company goals.

6. Establish the philosophy that good management is the development of people, not the direction of things. Aim at developing the whole person.
7. Teach key personnel the management techniques of research, planning, organization, direction, coordination, and control.
8. Motivate people by—
   a. Fulfilling basic needs for security, opportunity, recognition, belonging, and significance.
   b. Expecting their best—within reason.
   c. Positive listening and a positive mental attitude.
   d. Building on strengths.
9. Develop the realization that work can and should be a pleasant and rewarding part of life.
10. Establish the belief that integrity is the most important ingredient in all human activity.

Some Do's and Don'ts

Clearly, these ten steps cover every aspect of the manager's job. They also reflect the weaknesses and needs we have noted in the business environment today, and they make very specific demands on the individual executive in his relations not only with subordinates but with fellow managers as well.

First, some don'ts:

Don't talk about yourself any more than you need to. The feeling among your people that you have a "we" team is important. Far from making you a weaker executive, it strengthens your position in every way. You serve notice that you are a big enough person not to overuse the word "I" just to bolster a sagging sense of confidence.

Don't be negative. How do you like being around a negative thinker? Perhaps, after a meeting or conversation with a particular individual, you have been left feeling slightly depressed or thoroughly unsettled. Careful review will usually show that the other man expressed a number of negative views. This can have a chilling effect on real creative productivity.

Don't knock your subordinates or your "competitors"—ever.

Don't be overly diplomatic or sugary. A phony will always be spotted. If you acquire a reputation as a boss who wants to make everybody feel good no matter what happens, your potential effectiveness begins to decrease and will continue to decrease until you decide to face up to people and talk problems through.

Don't try to "manipulate" people. Who wants to be "manipulated"? Manipulators are phonies—and phonies finish last.

Don't say anything to a subordinate you can't say sincerely. The top executive sets the tone for the entire organization; if he's not sincere, he's asking for a group of yes men around him, people with neuroses, and for high executive turnover.

Don't yield to the temptation to be a yes man yourself. Your boss will see through you as easily as you see through your subordinates.

Don't be an appeaser. This is only a stopgap measure; usually you find yourself behind the eight ball if you don't meet a problem head on.

Don't be sarcastic. All sarcasm stems from a focus on weaknesses.

Don't forget the other person's point of view.

Don't confuse activity with results. You may put in 40 hours' work a week, but what does the company get out of it?

Don't react unwisely when you encounter apathy. It *is* disturbing, but there is usually a reason for it, and you may be that reason.

And on the positive side:

Help other people see the benefit—to them—of your order or suggestion.

Discuss performance, not personality, when you counsel subordinates.

Be positive but not dogmatic; candid but not blunt.

Aim at consistency. "That hard-headed old character may be tough to work for, but, by gosh, he doesn't play any favorites!"

Be objective. All decisions are *subjective*—but should be based on *objective* information.

Know your subordinates' strongest motivations.

Reflect honesty and sincerity in all your dealings.

Practice human kindness as well as tough-mindedness.

Demonstrate those virtues you advocate.

Let your enthusiasm show.

Recognize the power of questions, and *listen*.

Search for their strengths.

Top Management Lays the Keel

The responsibility for developing a climate of productivity lies squarely with top management.

To begin with, the chief operating executive must have a thorough idea of the kind of person he himself is. He may be benevolent, oily, diplomatic—or autocratic, cold, austere, and unbending. He may be just a "nice guy," willing to do almost anything to keep his subordinates from getting angry with him. He may be the autocratic type, the bull-of-the-woods who believes in one-man rule. Occasionally he may be full of fears: of subordinates, of progress, of life itself. If he has been exposed to the latest management thinking, he may be democratic, permissive; he will undoubtedly stress group responsibility and group decision making. Ideally the executive will be candid, fair, positive, vigorous; he will encourage genuine participation but retain final responsibility for the profit or loss resulting from over-all management decisions. And of course it's possible for a boss to combine these various traits; to be autocratic one day and permissive the next, keeping his subordinates in a state of angry confusion.

A book could be written about all these managerial types, but we are concerned here only with the leader who is candid, fair, positive, and vigorous—that is, the tough-minded manager. In setting out to establish the motivational climate, he must first insure that his immediate subordinates are made of the right stuff.

Are they psychologically attuned to their major roles? If the treasurer cherishes a secret yearning to be vice president of marketing, the president needs to know it. If the personnel director has always wanted to be a purchasing agent, his boss needs to know that too. Do the company's executives as a group have vitality, confidence, and a belief in our free enterprise system? Further, do they see an important role for the company in our free enterprise system? Can they change, grow, and stretch, or do they seek only a comfortable niche? How do they evidence integrity? Do their actions substantiate their words? (Pay no attention to lip service.)

Most important, what is wanted from each person? Following the development and refinement of over-all company objectives, a new organization alignment is sometimes necessary. Each major function must be required to accomplish certain specific results on both a short- and a long-term basis. For example:

Function	1st Year	3rd Year	5th Year
Director of marketing	Image study	Establish 40 retail outlets	Increase sales volume 20 percent
Director of manufacturing	Reduce costs 15 percent	Acquire half a million square feet of manufacturing space	Fully automate plant in Tennessee
Director of personnel	Establish profit-sharing plan	Set up management development program for all subsidiaries	Negotiate three-year contracts with all bargaining units
Controller	Establish budget department	Install profitability accounting in all work units	Establish company-wide profit plan
Director of research engineering	Build new test cell	Develop performance yardsticks for technical personal	Offer products powered by solar energy

In activating the motivational climate, the end results required in connection with each major objective should be set forth in clear statements of performance requirements. The term "performance standards" is of course commonly used, but personally I tend to avoid it, since in my experience management personnel often associate "standards" with piece work and other somewhat narrow concepts of management as a quantitative, antiseptic sort of activity. In any event, each department head should prepare the essence of such a statement in full awareness that he must justify its contents to his superior in terms of both the department's contribution to the company and the weekly, monthly, or quarterly control procedures which will normally be set up. The department head should then carry out this same process with key personnel all the way down in the organization. The considerations to be used as guides should always include:

People, Money, Materials, Time, and Space
and
What, Where, When, Who, How, and Why.

It cannot be emphasized too often that the only reason for being on a payroll is to contribute to organizational objectives. In judging the value of a subordinate, don't be swayed by old school ties and fraternities, club memberships, faultless attire, glibness, wit and charm, impressive vocabulary, long years of service, long hours (particularly without results), such paper qualifications as academic degrees, and other evidences of activity only. The person must be getting something done that directly or indirectly is moving the organization toward its goals. Without this, the rest is window dressing.

And what of accountability for results? By "accountability" we mean the clear understanding that a person does his job or gets out of it. This policy is in no way harsh or unjust if these self-evident conditions have been met: Is he *fully* trained for the job? Does he have a clear-cut accountability agreement which spells out the results he must achieve? Do you know what his personal goals and ambitions are? Has he been told about your goals for the company (or department) and, to some extent, your own personal goals? Does he have a definite part in determining or revising company goals, particularly in his own area—marketing, production, finance, or the like? Have you taken the time to become well acquainted with him personally? Is *your* example what it ought to be? Have you told him privately just what you feel his strengths and weaknesses are—with emphasis on his strengths? In short, does he know the *what, where, when, who, how,* and *why* of his job? And, finally, does he receive all the operating data he needs—on costs, scrap, turnover, absenteeism, and so on? If you can answer yes to all these questions, you are not only justified in holding him accountable for real accomplishment but obligated to do so.

All managerial and supervisory personnel must realize why "management is the development of people rather than the direction of things." This statement is being articulated increasingly by top executives of real growth organizations. It is, to be sure, the kind of statement, or credo, that many give testimony to but fail to follow through by actual practice and example. Yet we can reasonably say that it is a common denominator in the top management philosophy of every organization whose success has been truly outstanding. To illustrate: George I. Long, Jr., past president of the Ampex Corporation, said: "Since objectives are achieved by *people,* an atmosphere that will encourage individuals to operate at their optimum ability should be created within the company. Procedures for determining the extent of accomplishment are essential, as is a well-conceived compensation program that will reward outstanding performance by individuals and groups."*

*AMA Management Report No. 44 (1960), p. 23.

The motivational climate, then, requires a mandate to the rest of the organization that this philosophy will be followed in word and deed. Such a statement might read as follows:

It is the policy of this organization that all members of management and supervision shall consider the full development of their subordinates an important and essential requirement of their positions. From time to time they will be required to show evidence of adherence to this policy. . . .

Following up the companywide dissemination of a thoughtfully prepared philosophy, it is obviously necessary to establish development procedures to teach the fundamentals of the productivity climate. The general skeleton of a development program should be built around the six steps in the management process: (1) research, (2) planning, (3) organization, (4) direction, (5) coordination, and (6) control. These steps are an outline at best. The basic subject matter should suggest the do's and don'ts listed in Chapter 21.

Above all, key personnel should understand the fundamentals of motivation. Here it will pay to keep in mind the six steps just cited:

Research. Make use of attitude surveys, interviews, questionnaires, psychological testing.

Plan. Learn how to transmit objectives downward in the most meaningful way.

Organize. Set up suitable facilities; combine all logistic requirements; choose cases, incidents, other illustrations. Know what strengths are available.

Direct. Hold meetings and/or make and keep appointments with subordinates. Communicate clear and stretching expectations.

Coordinate. Counsel subordinates; show the relationships between corporate and personal goals. Stress and exemplify the stimulating and life-preserving values of work and the indivisibility of "getting a lot done" and "having fun."

Control. Measure results; determine increases in contribution.

Key personnel should understand further how communication pervades every facet of business. In the motivational climate nobody can *assume* that he is understood. How many times have you said, or heard someone say, "I wrote you a memo. I *assumed* you understood." Or, "I *told* you when the shipment was due." And so on. Such failure in communication encourages buck passing, office politics, and the proliferation of unnecessary paperwork. The operations manager of a large and relatively autonomous Midwestern plant with headquarters in New York recently stated that 80 percent of the memoranda received from the New York office were intended purely for purposes of self-protection. The tough-minded executive will not tolerate this situation.

Here are some pointers on this vital ingredient of the motivational climate:

- Proper grammar, good vocabulary, and pear-shaped tones do not insure communication (though everyone realizes the negative effect of a hopelessly illiterate memo). They only accomplish satisfactory transmission of an idea, thought, or order.
- Communication is complete only when the recipient knows what you mean and reacts in the way you desire.
- If the recipient does not react in this way, you must assume that you did not communicate well and blame yourself instead of the other person. Consider carefully the ramifications of this approach as applied to an entire department or organization. It is not easy. It requires a kind of tough-mindedness and self-discipline that quickly shows whether you are a big or a little person. The big person quickly perceives that this is an excellent, although arduous, way to—
  1. Eliminate buck passing. Pointing your finger at the other person just isn't done in the motivational climate.
  2. Eliminate politics. People can't very well "work on each other" in this climate.
  3. Clear up jealousies. The motivational climate must be a wholesome environment free from knives in the back.

And these are only a few of the many benefits which accrue when people's minds are free from anxiety and ready for productivity; when work is valued as an essential part of living; and when management's every action bears out the sincere belief that integrity is the most important ingredient in the business spectrum.

The Taut Ship

For many years the caliber of naval and merchant marine captains was measured by their ability to run a taut ship. At the risk of being redundant, I shall list here the essentials of the taut ship. All employees should understand—

What	the job is all about;
	is right—or wrong;
	should be done;
	shouldn't be done.
Where	the company has been;
	the company is going;
	new markets, products, and processes are coming from;
	the work should be done.
When	goals must be met.
Who	works for whom;
	does what for whom;
	should be contacted;
	should be informed.
How	best to do the job.
Why	the company is in business;
	the department is in operation;
	the job is required;
	the present method is used—

Plus many other *what's, where's, when's, who's, how's,* and *why's* as appropriate.

Do you *care* enough about your people to search out their strengths—their best possibilities—and *expect* their best?

3

Decide what you want!

Performance Is All
That Matters

To declare that performance is all that matters sounds a little rigid and unbending at first glance. What about values? What about altruism? What about being one happy family in jolly good fellowship? What about service to community and country?

The term "performance" actually encompasses all of these things. Our concern here, however, is with more than a definition of values. We need to discuss what to *do* about them. You must decide what you want the performance of your subordinates to yield. Ask yourself squarely, then, why you are in business:

To produce a greater return on investment?
To increase net profit?
To create new things?
To improve service to consumers?
To market a better product?
To bring in new customers?
To provide leadership?
To build a personal estate?

To retire at an early age?
To turn management over to younger people?
To develop a corporate image?
Other reasons?

This requires of course, that we determine company goals and relate personal goals to them. But inspiring the needed quality of performance means still another set of problems, many of them people-oriented.

Dangers of "Realism"

In just about every staff or production meeting or board room you will find the innovator and the "abominable no man"—and types who are somewhere in between. Here are some of them:

1. The bright-eyed zealot who feels that anything connected with growth and newness must be good, regardless of cost or net profit.
2. The person who waits for the boss to tip his or her hand so that he can agree. This kind of person is gutless.
3. The suave individual who makes progressive-sounding comments, uses the word "dynamic" often, and contrives largely to hold his job.
4. The tough-minded person who demands facts, a blueprint for action, realistic controls, is impatient to get something done and insists on involvement, commitment, and conviction.
5. The individual who is opposed to innovation of any kind if it involves courage and positive action. His usual reaction to new ideas is, "Come on, now, let's be *realistic*."

There are fine shadings between these five types. At the moment, however, we want to know what can be done about the last one.

Obviously there is a need for sound, realistic data prior to activating a program or plan. Companies have gone bankrupt owing to euphemistic daydreams without any foundation of facts. But more companies have failed to grow, or failed altogether, because innovation was stifled.

Innovation is often thought of as limited to new products. This is far too narrow a concept. Innovation may refer as well to new equipment, new policies and procedures, new people, new organizational structure, new distribution outlets, new plants, new layouts, new budgets and controls, new contracts, new records, new forms, and, above all, new *ideas*.

I have already recommended that the negative personality who hides behind a façade of "realism" be counseled on his net contribution to the company and be given a stipulated period of time in which to change or be dismissed. This sounds unfair, but it isn't. Such a person, if unable to change, will be happier in a different environment.

Incidentally, I do not mean to impugn here the role of the capable, informed controller. While it has been traditional for financial executives to sit on the purse strings, many are now beginning to install such innovations as profit planning and profitability accounting, with the result that the financial function is becoming truly valuable to the growing, profitable business.

So—get rid of the obstacle builders and staff up with solution finders, in the finance department or anywhere else.

The Only Reason for a Salary

I have stated that the only reason for receiving compensation from a business is adequate performance; that is, contribution to the accomplishment of company objectives. What weight, you may ask, should be given to good intentions? To seniority? To personal need?

These questions are not easy to deal with in a way that will be meaningful to everyone. I remember a department head who had been counseled several times on his failure to meet commitments and who was called in to be dismissed. He was hurt and surprised; his sole purpose and desire, he said, had been to please his boss. There was no question about this—he had even emptied the boss's ashtray on occasion! Furthermore, he had a large family, and he couldn't meet basic expenses for more than a short time if unemployed.

Such a situation has saved many jobs in many companies for many men. The soft-minded manager often defers direct action in the hope that the situation will remedy itself. This is the easy way. However, the procrastinating executive must be made to realize that it almost always hurts more people than it helps. Here are some results of indecision and procrastination:

1. Productive employees resent nonproductive employees' lack of contribution.

2. The paths of promotion and advancement become clogged with incompetents.
3. Because soft-minded people surround themselves with softer-minded people, the barrel fills with mushy apples.
4. The soft-minded people themselves are not comfortable in the long run. Unless they change—and they often can—they suffer, and their families and friends suffer.
5. Capable young people still in a malleable state are affected by what they see. If non-productive people are allowed to remain, these capable young people either leave or—worse yet—change. They grow slack and become indecisive, negative sycophants.

The policy which states that remuneration must be related directly to contribution is fair. So is the rule that calls for dismissing the person who—after suitable counseling—still is not contributing properly to the accomplishment of company objectives. Tough-minded subordinates want it this way. People who are not sure of themselves sometimes do not, although the motivational climate has converted many people from ambivalence to productive, satisfying toughness.

Making Things Happen

Imagine that you are looking down on a major city from the air and can see into 500 staff meetings. In the majority of cases, you will see one or the other of these two general patterns of action:

The boss asks for comment and questions but gets very little reaction. He phrases his own questions so that a "yes" or "no" is indicated. One or two intrepid souls voice a thought or two; and, if the boss does not express approval, the others assume that they should politely attack the ideas brought forward. The boss pulls everything together and sums up what he had in mind originally. Assignments are then made, and these are deliberately executed in a manner calculated to please the boss. Nothing extra is put into them because there was no initial feeling of participation. The same process is repeated next week.

The boss has to rap for order—and it turns out that he has no real agenda. There is much discussion in a truly permissive atmosphere. The resources needed to carry out proposed projects are considered with a fair degree of thoroughness. Assignments are made, each person being asked to do his best. These assignments are undertaken with good intentions, but the results don't quite measure up. The boss is vaguely dissatisfied, but he can't say much because the people obviously work hard and with enthusiasm. Again, the same process is repeated next week.

What does it take, then, to make things happen?

1. Each staff member attending a meeting should receive a copy of the tentative agenda and should himself determine the contribution he can make to the meeting's objectives and decide what results he would like to see achieved.
2. This information should be collated into a master agenda.
3. At the beginning of the meeting, the chairman or senior executive should clearly lay out the end results that are generally felt to be desirable.
4. An atmosphere of candor is essential; however, it must stress not what is wrong with an idea but what could be *more right*.
5. When a criticism is expressed, it should be accompanied by an alternative recommendation.
6. Evasive or meaningless conversation which does not bear on the subject at hand should be discouraged.
7. The problem-solving process should be used extensively:
    a. Define the problem. Precisely where are we now?
    b. Establish objectives. What do we want to do?
    c. Get the facts. Consider personnel, money, materials, time, and space.
    d. Weigh and decide. Look at the whole picture.
    e. Take action. Otherwise all else is futile.
    f. Evaluate the action. Was it effective? How could it have been improved?
8. Place time and quantity controls on all assignments.
9. Hold each person accountable for end results.

A highly useful tool for individual planning and control is a simple sheet with the following headings: "Specific Objectives," "Personnel Requirements," "Financial Requirements," "Material, Equipment, and Facilities Requirements," "Policy and Procedural Requirements," "External Conditioning Factors," "Action Required," and "Target Dates (Beginning and Completion)." The tough-minded manager can use one of these sheets for each major objective in his company or department—in preparation for a forthcoming meeting or not—and feel sure that it will aid him greatly in running a taut ship.

"Nice Guy" Management

What is a "nice guy"? Certainly not the reverse of a bad or dishonest guy. In sharp contrast to the tough-minded manager, the nice guy conditions most of what he says and does by his own emotions. While he makes a fine friend and neighbor, he often isn't equal to the demands of a management position.

Many nice guys have great difficulty realizing that the net result of doing the gentle or bland thing in the purported interest of the subordinate's or the boss's feelings is just the opposite of their goal. Yet dealing evasively and nicely with a man when frankness is needed is downright dishonest; you are failing to give him credit for basic dignity. The nice guy is often heard to say: "I like him too well to hurt him." Unfortunately, in the long pull, that is just what you do when you beat around the bush. This kind of management is selfish; you are sparing your own feelings at the other person's expense.

In many instances, a psychiatrist cannot make progress with a patient while the relationship between them is one of friendliness and informality. Real therapy sometimes begins only when the patient is disturbed by the psychiatrist's probing for truth and becomes angry.

It goes without saying that the need for candor in the motivational climate should never be construed as license for harshness or brutality. When all the components of this climate are present (with emphasis on basic needs), directness and truthfulness should never be anything but constructive.

The "Methods Improvement" Panacea

I have talked to many methods engineers, procedures analysts, systems experts, and others in the same general category. They often seem to have the same lament: "How can I get management to buy this idea?"

The chief methods engineer in a metal-fabricating plant told me once that he was about to resign. Why? Because the resident manager didn't want better methods, he wanted more accountants but didn't know it. I asked the engineer what that meant. He sputtered,

"Every time I need a final O.K. on a new improvement project, the fellow wants to know what it will contribute to *profit*. Hell, that's *his* job—and the job of the people in Accounting! I'm an engineer!"

This is no isolated case. It is, in fact, easy for management to point an accusing finger at the many people who are devising procedures for the sake of the procedures and to shake its collective head despairingly. Let's take a look, however, at the environment management frequently creates for these people:

1. No knowledge of company objectives.
2. No method of assessing their contribution to those objectives.
3. No relationship between actual contribution and compensation; rewards for length of service rather than results.
4. No relationship between actual contribution and advancement; promotion of the person with several degrees to the exclusion of the less highly educated person who may be making the greater contribution.
5. Emphasis on quantity and format in the preparation of procedures.
6. No systematic review and appraisal of contribution and personal development.
7. No current, accurate picture of the company's status.
8. No feeling of participation in departmental planning and decision making; consequent lack of recognition, security, and belonging.

For a stretching environment within the climate of motivation, these conditions must be righted. A shift in semantics is often helpful:

Not this, but	*This*
Budget	Profit plan
Cost center	Profit center
Suggestion system	Contribution (or profit improvement) system
Cost control	Cost improvement
Historical accounting	Profitability accounting

In summary, it is necessary to recognize the differences among analysis, evaluation, execution, and synergistic achievement. *Analysis* simply means to break an operation down into its component parts. Many methods people have stopped at this point. *Evaluation* means placing a value on the components and putting them back together, then determining the new values, if any, which exist. Other methods improvement people have stopped at this second point. *Execution* means doing something about the evaluation—taking action. *Synergistic achievement* is the only justifiable reason for doing any of the other three things.

It is axiomatic, then, that the methods improvement practitioners can make an outstanding contribution to their companies only if they carry out studies and analyses designed to contribute directly to improvement in the performance of their employers. The tough-minded manager will not buy anything less and, at the same time, will recognize the importance of his own role. John D. Staley put it well when he said:

> Without a doubt, the most important single ingredient in programming methods improvement is the determination of the manager to make his program work and to make it work *through the efforts of his people.* The degree to which this will-to-accomplish is present determines the extent of all the barriers to accomplishment. For the lazy manager, the obstacles are truly insurmountable. For the uncertain manager, however cost-minded, who doubts that he can do what is required, methods improvement will be well-nigh impossible. For the competent, determined individual, on the other hand, the most valuable satisfaction will come, not from the mere receiving of rewards, but from the certain feeling that these rewards have been earned and shared.[1]

Return on Investment—Fact or Fallacy?

I was amazed recently to note, in reviewing a dozen texts on management, that return on investment was not shown in the index of any of them. This is a bit hard to justify, since one of the fundamental goals of a publicly owned corporation is to offer stockholders a suitable return for the money they have made available. It is, however, altogether too typical of the conversation and writings of many past and contemporary management scholars. The emphasis is on the action involved rather than the end result desired.

Let us recognize that a fair return on investment is an integral part of our capitalistic system. Moreover, we should be proud enough of the way that system works to acknowledge the fact and to

[1] John D. Staley, *The Cost-Minded Manager,* American Management Associations (1961), pp. 162–163.

explain the *why* of it to workers. This is basic to effective communication and motivation.

On the other hand, there is an increasing tendency to judge the ability of managers by using return on investment as the sole criterion of performance. This is naïve on the surface of it. Any manager can slash costs to the bone—for example, by cutting staff services, including research and development—with a consequent increase in return to the investor. The long pull under these circumstances, however, can be disastrous to the company.

Excesses can be avoided with sound control by the board of directors.

Court of Appeal

Peter Drucker has said: "The Board cannot and must not be the governing organ that the law considers it to be. It is an organ of review, of appraisal, of appeal. Only in a crisis does it become an organ of action—and then only to remove existing executives that have failed, or to replace executives who have resigned, retired or died. Once the replacement has been made, the Board again becomes an organ of review."[2]

Very few boards of directors are currently exercising control over their companies' affairs to the full legal limits of their authority. I propose, therefore, that we staff our boards with capable, energetic people, getting rid of figureheads, and that they implement tough-minded management by—

1. Determining what stockholders *really* want.
2. Fulfilling these wants if feasible.
3. Giving the chief executive full cooperation but
4. Holding the individual accountable for results:
    a. What is the projected return on investment for, say five years? Why?
    b. What is the current status of established objectives?
    c. What is the company's current share of the market? What will it be next year? In five years?
    d. What progress is being made in other phases of planning?
5. Using return on investment as a performance yardstick.

[2] Peter F. Drucker, *The Practice of Management,* Harper & Row (1954), p. 179.

Strange as it seems, there are a great many boards that have no equivalent of a position description. Every person is a director and, as such, helps direct the business but very often cannot say toward what end.

It is important, clearly, that the top operating or executive executive—usually the president—not abdicate his responsibility by taking numerous operating decisions to the board. I have known many such timorous executives who felt this was a good way to curry favor. The proper kind of board will hand problems right back to the president—and, if he won't accept them, get a new president.

Again, the manager who simply seeks to make people "feel good" by obsequious or "nice" behavior does not merit a place on the payroll.

It is essential that the tough-minded interpretation of "performance" be fully understood.

Performance means the *total* performance of the person and includes as much emphasis on qualitative indices of performance as on the quantitative. For instance, real and satisfying quantitative results will simply not take place without a high, even excellent, measure of qualitative indices like commitment, confidence, courage, integrity, loyalty, hard work, fairness, judgment, and uncommonly good common sense.

4 *Where from? Where to?*

What Is Development?

A LOT of so-called management development has gone on during the past 20 years, and many of us have acquired a healthy skepticism about the demonstrated value of much that has been done in its name. Perhaps this is because few companies have stopped to determine whether they want to "train" or "develop" managers.

What is the difference between training and development? Training we can interpret to mean the orderly and systematic transmission of organized knowledge from one party or parties to another party or parties. This is often accomplished by rote, and it can result in an orderly feedback, or parroting, of just what the recipient has been told. However, it is *not* development. Development occurs only when—

1. Learning or modification of behavior takes place and
2. This is expressed in the application of changed and expanded attitudes and actions to achieve results.

The principal difference is that training stresses the *what* of a thing and sometimes the *how,* but for real development the *why* must be understood.

The Structured Approach

Drop in on the wide variety of "developmental" meetings being held throughout American organizations and you will all too often see an uncertain mishmash of tools, techniques, devices, and gimmicks in operation. These include—to name only a few—role playing, buzz sessions, case studies, brainstorming, sensitivity training, problem solving, the "inbasket" technique, and management "games," not to mention some more modish therapies like TA, TM, est, orgone, Rolfing, bio-energetics, Arica, scientology, and primal scream. Some of them actually produce a little development, though not too much.

It is often like trying to pour a quart of liquid into a pint. You waste time and liquid, and you don't expand the pint. The job in management development, of course, is just that: to expand the pint!

What It Adds Up To

Andrew Carnegie said many years ago: "Take away our factories, take away our trade, our avenues of transportation, our money. Leave us nothing but our organization, and in four years we shall have re-established ourselves."

"Organization" literally means people who are working together to accomplish something. Even when the thing to be accomplished is not clearly known, you have an organization, but it cannot be really effective. For true effectiveness, people must know where they are going and why. Hence management development.

In too many instances, however, the top executive or the board decides it is time to start a program. After all, everybody is getting into development, so there has to be some reason for it. A person must then be placed in charge of the program. Sometimes he is a capable professional, and sometimes he is simply the person nobody can find any other use for. He usually begins by reading the available materials and—at one time or another and often in a haphazard way—experiments with the usual tools and techniques: the organization manual, job rotation, management apprenticeships, a junior board of directors, assorted training devices (whichever are currently popular), performance appraisals, and executive counseling.

The tough-minded executive will quickly see that all of these tools add up simply to an attempt to give each person the *what, where, when, who, how,* and *why* about himself, his job, and the company. Why, then, haven't many company programs become dynamic *instruments* of management?

One reason is that we still view them as programs, projects, efforts, discrete areas of activity. We must see instead that sound, effective management growth cannot be isolated from other parts of the business; that, pervading as it does every segment of the company, it flourishes best where a total climate has been created. It should be clear that one of the end results of the motivational climate is development, and of the most positive kind. A systems approach is needed.

Opportunity to Stretch

The components of a lean and pointed approach to management development have been implied in previous chapters. Let's review them briefly with the specific needs of the development program in mind.

1. The appropriate executive, in articulating his fundamental beliefs, must stress the fact that the most important responsibility of all managerial and supervisory personnel is the development of people to better achieve the company's objectives. This step is vital. A statement that is half-hearted and doesn't appear to mean business can make the whole thing abortive. It should be skillfully worded, personally signed, and elaborated upon in all suitable media.

2. There should be no question that key personnel are thoroughly aware of over-all organization objectives. In a recent two-part seminar, I assigned the participants the project of securing statements of company objectives from their superiors during the month between sessions. Most of the people discovered that such statements were not available—but they were told to persevere. Indirectly they forced their top managements to do some very necessary thinking, with the result that everyone concerned experienced some significant growth, insight, and development.

3. The specific objectives of the management development function should be studied for agreement with company objectives. Objectives should be much more value-oriented than technique-oriented. They should focus on the qualities which really distinguish the pros from the amateurs.

4. It is obvious, that you can't make a silk purse out of a sow's

ear. You can't build a Shetland pony into a Percheron stallion. Therefore, with the preceding three steps under control, you must find out what kind of clay you have to mold; that is, you must make an inventory of existing manpower and evaluate its potential from the standpoint of present and future management needs. If your analysis is sufficiently satisfying, you need not be concerned with the next step.

5. Outside recruitment is of course necessary if jobs cannot be filled from within the company. Probably, in any case, it is good to have an injection of new blood now and then.

In recruiting and screening management personnel, five factors are important: values and beliefs, physical attributes and characteristics, abilities and skills, interests, and personality traits. Of these, *values and beliefs* are by all means the most vital; an abundance of other qualifications is futile without a drive for self-realization and achievement, faith in the dignity of man, and some idea of human problems and needs in the world arena. It is imperative that these values exist in at least a budding state in the person who you want to see develop and become truly broad-gauge. When you staff your organization with this kind of person you may find you'll have to develop higher, more stretching objectives.

Physical attributes and characteristics should perhaps be given greater weight here than in other environments. And anyone who is organically sound and free of disease can and should strive for a high measure of physical fitness. So look for the clear-eyed, flat-bellied person. Many top executives agree that the relatively young person who carries a roll of suet around his middle probably won't stand up to the requirements of long hours and split-second thinking as well as his fit and hard counterpart. Moreover, he will very likely prefer the easier course of action, regardless of performance criteria.

Abilities and skills may or may not be reflected by scholastic achievements. Professors of business administration often try scrupulously to steer prospective employers away from young people who have made a habit of cutting classes, who prefer extracurricular interests, whose grades are not outstanding—and from the nonconformist who may, for example, have headed some minority group on campus. This policy should not go unchallenged: Experience has shown that many of the most capable executives and innovators deviate widely from the "ideal" pattern, and there are excellent students who simply cannot make the transition to the business world.

Use your common sense, then. Grades are important, but hiring management trainees solely on the basis of their Phi Beta Kappa keys can be a real mistake.

Interests, as indicated by tests, interviews, and statements on application forms, should be reasonably well related to the nature of the company. Personality traits, finally, are the mortar in the chimney. The quality of the bricks will be meaningless unless they are properly cemented. Intelligence, appearance, and experience will be of no use to you without good personal and social adjustment.

6. Organization planning must many times precede the initial awareness of the need for management development. In any case, however, it is vital to the growth-oriented company, and the very process of participating in it serves to develop all those who are charged with formulative responsibility. Organization planning provides direction, purpose, and control where drifting might otherwise become habitual.

7. Really tough-minded organization planning also forces the determination, clarification, and revision of objectives, where appropriate, whether for company, division, department, section, or individual.

8. Because it is important that each person know how he is doing—not just from the standpoint of meeting performance requirements but to improve strengths and eradicate weaknesses—the construction of rating scales and sheets used in the appraisal process is far less crucial than the counseling which follows. Performance-appraisal counseling is one way to bring about *development of the whole person.* Focusing on accomplishments, hidden strengths, and unrealized potential is an approach which has a high yield. Focusing on weaknesses compresses the individual and seldom results in "stretch." The tough-minded manager permeates his whole philosophy with an emphasis on strengths and attainable results, on the opportunity to stretch and grow.

9. Similarly, accountability must be viewed as the gadfly in the productivity climate. It should not and cannot be properly installed and enforced unless preceded by two main essentials: (1) performance requirements which provide stretch and (2) fulfillment of people's basic needs. These give you pull and substance; with accountability added you have push and stimulation.

A food-processing company decided it would hold all its key personnel accountable for results. The top executive, however, was a "nice guy" who shortly began to allow for various extenuating circumstances. Soon it became established procedure for his subordinates to report to his office claiming the most ingenious extenuations. This reduced the whole thing to a farcical procedure. When the chief finally was encouraged to develop a realistic but firm set of permissible extenuations—plus a number of other tough-minded innovations—the accountability program shaped up.

10. A sound scheme of executive compensation can be an integral part of management development; however, it certainly is essential to building and maintaining an effective management team and it is a widely discussed aspect of good management. Yet many companies, otherwise well run, operate by hunch and intuition in this area and wonder why executive turnover is so high. Numerous texts on job evaluation have had the net result of scaring companies away from using this important tool of salary administration in connection with executive personnel; they have made suggested plans sound hopelessly complex and involved. That these need not be complex at all has been proved many times in the motivational climate.

Separating the Pros from the Amateurs

What separates the adequate performer from the highly productive one? The highly productive person from the outstanding one? In numerous instances, I have watched the comparative growth and development of two people whose performance on psychological and intelligence tests was almost identical. The causative factors here defy precise definition and stem from a whole complex of circumstances.

Guts and heart. Many times I have felt strongly that the primary difference between two such people is intestinal fortitude, courage, or just plain guts. The ability, in other words, to react to adversity by coming back stronger than ever.

The executive vice president of a publishing firm was determined to find out who among his management trainees really had the grit to get the job done under stress. He devised a series of trying situations to test their mettle. One device involved calling someone out of bed at 2:00 a.m. to handle an emergency at the plant—a test which several failed by looking for any excuse not to show up in person. Extreme, perhaps, but the tough-minded executive knows that the untried person may fail the company at a critical time if he has not developed stamina and dependability.

Vision. Can a manager be taught to visualize the long-range requirements of his company or department, or is this something innate? Many people become expert technicians—that is, in market research, employment interviewing, job analysis, methods improvement, or cost accounting. They often achieve what appears to be real proficiency because they burrow down into small compartments of activity and knowledge by sheer exposure to them.

The young resident manager of a large and profitable tire-building plant once told me that his seven subordinates were about 15 years older than he, on an average, and that each knew more about his own function than the plant manager could hope to know. He pointed out that the principal advantage which had put him in his present job was a real thirst for seeing the total picture—he always wanted to know *why* a thing was done.

Vision may be partly an inborn trait, but it may be improved greatly by developing a curiosity about the world around you, business in general, and your company in particular. It is important in this connection to recognize that external factors beyond the control of company or individual have a major impact on much of what happens internally. Among these conditioning factors are social trends, economic developments, political events and changes, and competitive pressures.

Force, stretch, and creativity. The internal factors which generate forceful executive and worker habits can operate for the distinct good of the organization—or the opposite. We all have needs and drives. The important thing is that they be channeled toward those established objectives we have mentioned so often.

Force in the productivity climate may be defined as directed energy, movement, through dedication and belief, toward clearly understood and worthwhile goals. The relation of creativity to force should be apparent from the following example: A well-known firm of consulting management psychologists makes it a distinct point, in screening managerial applicants for client firms, to recommend only those people who manifest a high degree of personal and social adjustment—the kind who are pretty well contented with everything as it is. This is done deliberately "to keep from rocking the boat." Disagreements and arguments in client companies are quickly soothed and smoothed over. Conformity and permissiveness may not be goals, but they are the net result. For it is notable in many of this firm's client companies that innovation and growth have slowed up radically. Instead of everybody's being "happy," there are inhibitions and neuroses. Why? Because three things lacking are force, creativity, and stretch.

But you don't need force to be creative, someone may say. Aren't there some relatively unaggressive inventors?

I am discussing here a kind of internal charged current, or force, which gets its start in dissatisfaction with sameness and the status quo. A healthy measure of dissatisfaction should be encouraged throughout the key functions in any organization that is set up for accomplishment. While it is important to fulfill the basic needs of personnel, this should be done, not for the sake of producing satiation or bovine contentment, but to *develop* a greater hunger for achievement and contribution. Religious teaching in no way casts a reflection on ambition unless it is directed solely at self-aggrandizement. *It is virtually impossible to be too ambitious if your energies are pointed toward contribution, toward giving and building.*

Thus the motivational climate, which calls for stretching toward positive goals, must have both force and creativity. The tough-minded manager will take steps to unleash both in his subordinates or watch his competitors carry away the plums.

Growth Is Personal

One of the most frequent laments among managers who have experimented with management development programs is that the injection—or vaccination—of new knowledge doesn't "take." Here again we see the need for a total climate which lends itself to individual dignity, the fulfillment of basic needs, and gives a person the feeling that he is the master of his own destiny. To tell him constantly and benevolently what is good for him is to diminish him.

You cannot motivate a person, I repeat. You can only provide the environment, climate, or atmosphere that will help him supply and seek his own motives. People can be made to learn, but not by simply feeding them knowledge. Learning must usually take place within some kind of emotional context: that is, mixtures and combinations of enthusiasm, fear, joy, anxiety, grief, disappointment, hunger. This basic principle is widely misunderstood, and no one should attempt consciously to apply it without a measure of training. However, I have known several executives who provide the right climate for learning without even thinking of words like "emotional context," in most cases because they are so genuinely convinced of the benefit of their counsel, and so objective in giving it (or so interested in the other person to the exclusion of self), that these very qualities stimulate a wholesome emotional context and promote real learning.

In the final analysis, a person must see the advantage, to him, of learning. He must *want* to grow, or very little development will be accomplished.

The Elusive Essential

I have sometimes said the scarcest personal quality in our world today is genuine, deep, sustaining self-confidence. Look behind the behavior of the bully, the egotist, the show-off, the criminal, the whiner, the dictator, and you will almost always find a lack of belief in self—an insufficient awareness of one's own strengths.

Stop and reflect what kind of world this would be if everybody had a full measure of self-confidence. Wars, minority problems, murders, rape, slander, office politics would not exist. They would not exist because nobody would feel it necessary to prove anything to himself or others. Have you noticed that really confident people take their work seriously but not themselves? They get more done and have more fun.

Let's return for a moment to our recommendation to build on strengths instead of focusing on weaknesses. How often, in business, a person is reprimanded for what he did *wrong!* Usually this drains away a little more of his self-esteem, and his chances of improving are not greatly helped. However, when you tie in your suggestions or criticisms with reminders about how much *better* he can do, you begin to tap the deep well of potential that the average person seldom discovers in a lifetime.

Lack of self-esteem is at the bottom of the majority of business problems. The tough-minded manager learns that one of the most challenging and thrilling experiences in life is to develop ordinary people into extraordinary people. Here is a truly fine test of professionalism and stature in management.

Remember, the vital stuff, the constructive essence, in all people is the sum of their *strengths*. The tough-minded manager insists on finding all possible strengths in the person in the mirror, all possible strengths in his colleagues, and then he *expects* them to be used.

How many people have *you* helped build?

Plan for Accomplishment

For several years, planning—particularly long-range planning—has been a popular topic of conversation in management circles. Every progressive executive believes in planning; you can no more knock it than apple pie or the Constitution.

To listen in at management seminars, we might assume that there is a tremendous wave of effective planning surging ahead throughout business. This just isn't so! Digging beneath the surface and asking penetrating questions about the nature of some of these company plans, we see quickly that most of them are euphemistic conglomerations that contribute very little real clarity and purpose. Here is what often happens: The top executive "gets the word" on long-range planning. He knows it's great stuff; so he says to his staff in effect, "You fellows meet on Saturday morning and hammer out a set of objectives for us—and, if you have time, develop a long-range plan."

Many times such a hastily conceived batch of objectives will be produced in a few hours. The top executive will then tell his staff that they are responsible for getting them accomplished. Now they have long-range planning.

Why Don't We Plan More?

Psychologists and other researchers have told us that there is an innate human resistance to change. People want to live for today. Any hesitance to cast off into the unknown is normal. Not so.

This unfortunately applies to many people in our country today, but that is not to say it should continue to do so. A searching examination of the writings of the great philosophers reveals that growth, strength, and progress are closely dependent on planning, vision, and identification with the future. It is part of God's plan that productivity and a sense of happiness are to a great extent related to a series of anticipations and a quickened interest in tomorrow.

At a recent convocation of 36 companies which were represented by both top operating executives and board members, I asked why none of them had actually developed a master-planning blueprint. Hadn't they extolled the virtues of planning from *A* to *Z*? I probed and questioned until the group cut loose and responded vigorously. The reasons they gave for *not* planning, listed on a blackboard, boiled down to these: We don't have—

The information.
The imagination.
The initiative.
The guts.

This was not strictly true, of course. Many of the group had demonstrated all these qualities in abundance throughout other phases of management. What, then, was responsible for their state of mind?

Further questioning and analysis revealed that most of these people simply didn't have sufficient knowledge of the actual substance and specific processes involved in planning. A surprising dynamism ensued when this deficiency was remedied and materials and tools were made available to them.

To Get Participation and Cooperation

One approach to long-range planning is to determine what you want to accomplish over the next five or ten years in the following eight areas:

1. Innovation.
2. Market standing.

3. Manager performance and development.
4. Worker performance and attitude.
5. Physical and financial resources.
6. Productivity.
7. Public responsibility.
8. Profitability.

These are the areas in which, Peter Drucker[1] states, objectives of performance and results must be set. To do this brings the following sequence into play.

To begin with, all personnel down through the first level of supervision are asked to submit the results of their best thinking about the needs and goals of the organization for the coming five years. A time limit is set, and a real effort is made to convince people that their ideas will really be welcomed and that their opinions and front-line observations will be valuable. In smaller organizations it is sometimes possible to include every employee—bargaining unit and all—in this process. Amazingly positive results can accrue from the feeling of participation and identification which is thereby encouraged.

Next the accumulated data must be studied. This alone can be a real eye-opener for the average executive. He may wish to set up a series of convenient worksheets, several for each of the eight areas. Then, after careful analysis with the help of these sheets, candid discussion takes place among the staff, with the senior executive extracting and synthesizing comments, criticism, and recommendations. From this crucible comes the distilled wisdom of the business.

The top person should now have sufficient information to chart some definite goals. For example: "Increase sales 20 percent a year for five years." Or: "Provide a 12 percent return on investment." These objectives represent the best composite thinking of his management team—which, in itself, is more than most companies achieve.

The role of each division or department head must of course be clarified. The marketing chief, for instance, may develop specific goals directed toward the over-all objective of "increasing sales 20 percent a year for five years." Finally, all secondary-level executives follow a definitive blueprint for planning. For instance, in the De-

[1] Peter F. Drucker, *The Practice of Management,* Harper & Row (1954), pp. 62–87.

partment of the Air Force, this consists of an elaborately detailed procedure, somewhat condensed here:

1. Define and evaluate a series of specific objectives by using a succession of steps to establish a sequence of accomplishments.
2. Determine the elements in the situation or setting.
   a. For external conditioning factors determine the agencies and units [or, in industry, divisions and departments] which are directly involved.
   b. For internal conditioning factors:
      (1) Determine the resources needed.
      (2) Define in broad terms the techniques to be used.
      (3) Determine the pattern of flow of work.
      (4) Develop procedures and schedules of operations needed to reach each of the specific objectives.
      (5) Make provisions for adjustments when needed.
3. Determine patterns for control of operations.
4. Develop a panoramic view of the over-all pattern of the operational system, by ascertaining whether:
   a. The operational details cover the entire area.
   b. These details are consistent and compatible.
   c. The operation as detailed will contribute the maximum to over-all effectiveness.
5. Evaluate the anticipated contribution of the current needs of the organization.
   a. How closely will the results of planning approximate the purposes of the assigned objective?
   b. What conditions would make achievement of the objective more urgent?
   c. Under what conditions may the activity become superfluous?
6. Develop a detailed pattern of organizational structure.
7. Develop a detailed pattern for timely provision of material, facilities, funds, and personnel.
8. Visualize the procedural pattern to insure a smooth operation.
9. Develop required procedures not already in existence.
10. Develop some means of insuring compliance with the prescribed procedures.
11. Make provisions for integration of operations by:
    a. Adjusting the flow of supplies, availability of skills, and amount of manpower needed to meet operating changes in production.
    b. Fitting specific operations into the over-all production schedule.
12. Determine whether the relationships among the above elements are reasonable and practicable.
13. Consider whether the elements in the organization of operations form an operational system.
14. Determine which organizational elements are directly or indirectly

involved in the execution of specific steps in operation and the extent of such involvement.

15. Arrange means of insuring cooperation of these elements through:
    a. Proper liaison.
    b. Conferences and discussions.
    c. Formal and informal exchange of information.
    d. An understanding of common objectives.
16. Insure that proper channels for smooth flow of resources are cleared and known to personnel concerned.
17. Insure that:
    a. Actual work gets under way and progress is maintained.
    b. The elements of the organization perform in accordance with the plan and schedule.
    c. Production resources—manpower, material, and facilities—are integrated according to plan.
    d. Working procedures and performance requirements are clearly understood by personnel concerned.
    e. Compliance is indicated by meeting the requirements of quality, quantity, and time schedules.
    f. Necessary changes in operation are made smoothly, without disruption of production.
18. Conduct operations in accordance with the philosophy and policies of the organization.
19. Direct consistent efforts toward:
    a. Preservation of morale and working capacity of personnel, through training, recreation, and improvement in working conditions.
    b. Good publicity, wherever appropriate.
    c. Meticulous regard for safety of those involved in operations.
20. Seek possible improvements in operations.
21. Develop means for evaluating and, if feasible, measuring the progress of operations and the use of resources.
22. Determine means of evaluating control information.
23. Utilize planned corrective actions by:
    a. Removing bottlenecks.
    b. Replanning, reorganizing, and redirecting of operating elements.
    c. Evaluating results in terms of their solution of the problem.
24. Determine the extent to which operations are contributing to over-all effectiveness of the organization.

The Importance of Being Consistent

Perhaps the most important element of this system is that all personnel have a thorough understanding of *why* planning is so vital, *why* you are doing certain things, and *why* certain results are required of them.

As each of your subordinates moves into his particular area of planning responsibility, you must take care to maintain tough-minded, consistent controls. Otherwise he may develop a tendency to "put it off until I get my work done." Each person must realize that planning is an essential part of his work and that you are going to require periodic reports on progress—what the Department of the Air Force terms "well-documented, objective accounts of accomplishment."

The Vacillating Vice President

The marketing head of a well-known firm had moved up through the organization rapidly and achieved his vice-presidency at a relatively young age. He was a superb salesman—mentally alert, good-looking, and very voluble. As a vice president, however, he began to run into rocks and shoals. He had not submitted any reports to the president or completed any of his projects on schedule. Yet he seemed unperturbed; he was always too busy—always closing a big sale or thinking up a new idea which he personally wanted to try out. The president's patience was getting thin.

Few of the criteria of tough-minded management had been applied in this company. But, once a total planning program began to unfold and the components of the motivational climate were built in, the performance of the vacillating vice president began to improve rapidly. Here was another instance where an isolated series of reprimands and exhortations had no positive effect. Yet the motivational climate permeated and energized his understanding, and a potential failure was changed into a capable member of the management team.

Don't Listen to "Activity"

The effective leader is often impatient. However, an important distinction must be made between types of impatience. At his best, a leader is impatient not with the weaknesses of his subordinates but, rather, with the unused potential which is lying dormant in most of us. He is impatient with himself and is constantly looking for new ways to convert activity into results. He is always looking for new strengths in himself and others.

You may ask, "Does this mean that the tough-minded executive is an unhappy, abrasive fellow?" Quite the contrary! An impatience for positive, goals-oriented achievement is one of the soundest ways to bridge the chasm between emotional insecurity on the one hand and confidence, buoyancy, and self-assurance on the other.

If you have read carefully thus far, you should be able to tune in on a group of junior executives and spot the top person of tomorrow by picking the one who has the most of the following qualities:

1. Impatience for results.
2. A sense of purpose. He knows what he stands for—what he wants to get done.
3. A positive approach to problems.
4. The feeling that a problem can be solved until it has been proved otherwise.
5. Practical judgment. He sees the balance among men, money, materials, time, and space.
6. Familiarity with the "six honest serving men": *what, where, when, who, how,* and *why.*
7. Courage and candor.
8. A knowledge that all people need recognition, belonging, security, opportunity, and significance.
9. Acceptance of the fact that all projects of any significance involve planning, organization, coordination, direction, and control.
10. A tough, durable mind that refuses to dissipate mental, physical, and emotional energy on negative thinking.
11. A continuous search for strengths.
12. A zest for life, love, and wholeness.

What Do We Do About It?

Don't wait to start your planning program. If you hold back until you are meticulously prepared in every detail for the establishment of magnificent objectives—let's face it! You never will get started. The important thing is to set your goals and get the planning machinery under way. You must, of course, be impatient with your plans and their progress. But you won't have anything to refine and improve if you don't make a beginning.

Remember, too, that you need to condition your plans heavily with a thoroughly fortified knowledge of your consumer. Time and again companies have built a product and then—and only then—determined who wanted it and how to distribute it. This is asking for disaster. Base all your plans directly or indirectly on a well-researched fund of data about *what* the consumer wants, *where* he wants it, *when* he wants it, *who* he is, *how* he wants it, and—above all—*why* he wants it.

The tough-minded manager sets his ducks in a row, and then he *does* something about them.

In Chapter 21 we will explore specific requirements for a fully operational system of management by objectives.

6   *How do you energize the team?*

Organize for Results

ORGANIZING for results implies that you already know where you want to go and what you want to do there. It also implies that members of the management team understand their role in achieving this over-all goal.

The word "team" may have been overworked in management jargon, but it is still very apt. When two horses are harnessed together and then hitched to a heavy load, two things can happen: One horse may respond to your command first, and his forward lunge may throw the other horse back—even throw the slower animal off his feet. Or they may start simultaneously, in which case the one may pull harder later on but is unlikely to affect their joint performance. Individual effort, in other words, is generally futile even though occasionally brilliant. Your team of subordinate managers cannot be effective unless each person bears his full weight and pulls well in harness with the rest.

What It Takes

A manufacturer of electrical components decided to purchase, or build, a new facility in a Southern state. Typically, this assignment would be given to the vice president in charge of manufacturing, who would be held solely accountable for it from start to final activation. In this case he *was* charged with the responsibility, but the other vice presidents on the corporate staff were made accountable for clearly defined sub-results which were to be achieved by their divisions.

The top personnel executive had to produce manpower studies and data which tied direct dollars-and-cents savings to the advantages of locating in certain areas. The top marketing executive was accountable for information concerning the most logical distribution and sales procedures; the top financial executive was accountable for evaluating the past performance of business available for acquisition; and so on.

To make this pattern of accountability work, it was important that the president set forth each person's responsibility clearly—and so he did. If responsibilities are *not* set forth in unmistakable terms— if, for example, the president simply tells the chief manufacturing executive to take the ball and run with it—you have problems like these:

1. Finger pointing. "It's your job—the boss said so. I've got my own department to run."
2. Empire building. If you have no provision for necessary staff services and can't get them from appropriate departments, there is a tendency to hire people and build them into your own group. Tough-minded management cannot tolerate these layers of fat.
3. The feeling that the importance of your department is not recognized.

To energize the team, every key player must know the direction of the goal, the plays needed to get there, his role in each play, and the people, money, materials, time, and space required. It is crucial too that each team member feels identified with something bigger and more important than self.

Get Operational!

On many campuses, at the end of spring football training, we see more and more contests between the "varsity" and groups of returning alumni. There is something fascinating about these games to the student and practitioner of management. They are classic studies of the contribution that organization can make to success.

One Saturday I attended such a game. The alumni were two and three deep with players whose names are well known in professional football. Three of them held all-time school records, and one—an all-American with 11 years of pro football experience—held many national records. The varsity team had lost five games in the previous fall and had no all-American candidates in its ranks. In spite of past observations, there was still a tendency to feel that the potent aggregation of alumni talent just had too much for the younger and much lighter varsity.

The alumni held one drill and developed four basic plays, since time did not permit more. The young varsity players all knew the results expected of them, as well as the other players' roles and performance requirements. They were intimately acquainted with the resources available: the strengths and weaknesses of teammates, their own equipment and field, their regular coaches, and everything else which comprised a fund of sure, readily usable knowledge. They were *operational!* By the end of the game, the crowd had been treated to some brilliant individual efforts by alumni; however, while none of the varsity looked outstanding, the net result was a two-touchdown margin for them—and results were what they were there for.

The corporate trouble shooter, the management consultant, the chief executive himself—all must be adept at sensing the climate of the organization. Some teams are obviously dead and withering on the vine. The symptoms?

Passive resistance to change.
Apathy, indifference, listlessness.
Hostility; opposition to new things.
Extremes in emphasis on efficiency; that is—
  a. Gleaming, sterile, antiseptic offices and personalities. Every
     thing is stiff, formal, austere; everybody is called "Mr." and
     all three suit-coat buttons are fastened. Usually there is a
     surplus of memoranda. Or—
  b. Slovenly, informal, paper-littered desks; ashtrays full of cig-
     arette butts and lingering evidences of the coffee break;
     sloppy dress. Usually there should be *more* written memos.
Alcoholism; abnormal nervous tensions.
Ultra-sophistication; too much suave politeness.
Sarcasm and wit focused on the weaknesses of people and things.

How do you breathe new life into organizations that are drifting in this way? Here are just a few of the things that can be done (see also Chapter 2):

1. Rethink the basic purposes and objectives of the company and its people.
2. Determine where they are now—and why.
3. Set new goals: company, departmental, individual.
4. Take a fresh look at existing talent; use special abilities; identify present and potential strengths.
5. Insure efficient manpower balance; reduce where needed and staff up where needed.
6. Make certain that there is a *mutual* understanding of roles.
7. Examine the need for, and the usability of, available manpower tools: budgets, market research, procedures manuals, job descriptions, psychological testing, and the like.
8. Determine what has worked well in the past. Don't focus on past failures. Remain *un*satisfied rather than *dis*satisfied.
9. Insure that a comprehensive system of *expectations* is in operation.

Wasted Talents

Throughout America today we can see some truly sad examples of organizations which have outgrown people. There is the marketing executive who was the first good salesperson the company had. As the firm grew, the man didn't; and now that he is responsible primarily for sound management rather than personal salesmanship, he is lost. This is bad enough in itself, but it also results in stifling many good subordinates who either leave or, staying, settle for comfortable mediocrity.

Then there is the very real problem of how best to utilize the talents of people who differ from the majority in race, religion, or ideology. *This problem will continue to exist as long as we judge the individual by such criteria rather than performance.* It is far too easy to follow accepted practice, slough people off into general categories, and consider their talents and contributions limited accordingly. The tough-minded administrator faces up to this problem of prejudice instead of evading it. He has the courage to think for himself. He is committed to fairness above all else.

There is also the top executive who has come up through some specialty—say, marketing or finance—and refuses to let go of it; who fails to realize that the days of autocratic, one-man rule are past beyond recalling. And, of course, there is the self-made owner/manager who holds to the disappearing fallacy that the successful business calls for, and implies, a "strong man." The reverse is true. It takes no great strength to say, "You may do nothing without my approval. I built this business, and I alone have the answers." This is mere stupidity—an inability to recognize that none of us, as mortals, *can* have all the answers; that failure to face up to what our subordinates can do better may hurt many others.

The tough-minded manager knows that all a company's employees have something to contribute to it. He is not satisfied with less than an environment that uses each man's and each woman's contribution to further the goals of the business. It follows, naturally, that this also furthers the goals of the employee. He knows that commitment and conviction are not achieved without appropriate *involvement*.

The "We" Feeling

Some confusion exists about "I" and "we" in modern business. For instance, it is feared that the trend toward benevolent big government and toward conformist-type organization men will be stimulated by describing departmental and/or company actions as things "we" are going to do. The feeling is that this may restrain individuality. It is a thought that is worth examining closely, since the motivational climate needs—and develops—both strong individuals and cohesive group accomplishment.

First, intelligent self-interest and self-actualization are prerequisites to motivation, productivity, and generally good performance. To state the facts simply, a person will seldom put his best effort into a thing unless he sees the benefit to himself, even though he may be genuinely altruistic. A person cannot give himself totally to others, although most of his satisfaction may come from seeing the achievements of others; he vitally needs a strong feeling of *self*-achievement. (See Exhibit 1 in Chapter 20.)

Second, when a person is asked to make a contribution to a group effort that purports to be, and is continuously represented to be, the idea and passion of somebody else, it is basic to human nature that he will not give it his all. Third, the strong emergence of individuality will, accordingly, be hampered by the leader who talks about himself either directly or indirectly by making frequent use of "I," "my," and "mine."

Conversely, as is basic to the premises of tough-minded management, the kind of blossoming individuality stimulated by the motivational climate highlights the need for the "we" concept in developing people and achieving increasingly greater company goals. Intense competition among workers toward clearly defined targets fosters both individuality and total business success. Not competition with each other, but rather competition with one's own potential, one's own objectives and possibilities.

I have often noticed the tendency of some retail store clerks to say, "*I* am out of this material; *they* will have to order some." Or: "*I* don't have that kind of shoe in stock; *they* don't go in much for brown." Contrast the picture this generates with the spirit of the clerk who says: "*We're* out of this material. I don't know why, but *we* won't let it happen again."

In summary, the use of "we" by the top executive should never have the net effect of making subordinates feel "collectivized" if they see their own role clearly in the total enterprise. A strong and synergistic "we" must be the product of strong and actualized "I's".

Clear-cut Assignments

In the maze of internal memoranda, reports, and bulletins that is characteristic of many organizations, confusion is the rule rather than the exception. An approach that may be helpful in implementing the communications principles of the motivational climate urges all communicators to prepare their materials on the premise that "if it *can* be misunderstood, it *will* be misunderstood."

The technique of work assignment must, needless to say, vary sharply with the nature of the job and the caliber of the person. To assume that there is one best way that will work with all subordinates is a mistake. Rather, it is important to use the appropriate kind of written or spoken language. A janitor may require precise instructions on how thoroughly you want your office cleaned, how often, and how long the job should take. A vice president may need only to know that you expect a sales report by a certain date. He, however, must supply the *what, where, when, who, how,* and *why. Good* people usually heed directions. *Excellent* people usually heed only direction. They will supply their own *directions.*

Here are some examples of good and bad work assignments:

Good	Bad
"Bill, find out what's causing that scrap and tell me how much you can reduce it and when."	"Bill, we've got to reduce the scrap rate."
"You aren't meeting your commitment to hold the line on costs. Tell me why, and we'll see if we can figure out what needs to be done."	"The costs in your department are out of line. Let's get on the ball."
"This correspondence should be done by tomorrow noon—and remember, we can't send our customers any letters with errors, misspellings, or erasures."	"Your speed and accuracy are down—you've got to improve."
"Schedule a meeting of the Production Planning Committee in Conference Room B at 3:00. The meeting will last until we get that delivery problem solved."	"Better hold a meeting about that delivery problem."

The Delegating Executive

Reams of "literature" have been turned out concerning the principles and precise processes of delegation. Is it an involved and meticulous exercise? What does the tough-minded manager think?

The delegating executive must do five things:

1. Make sure that the written statement of the subordinate's responsibility, authority, and accountability is a product of thorough discussion with him. The head of a big organization may object that job descriptions, statements of responsibility, and performance requirements should be worked out by some staff department, but this kind of discussion between superior and subordinate is the essence of the management process. The appropriate staff department can assist with format and polishing.
2. Grant authority commensurate with the results required. Give the subordinate real backing in deed as well as word or you haven't really delegated, you have just sloughed off a problem temporarily.
3. See that the subordinate is accountable to one person only and

that he knows well the performance criteria by which he
will be judged.

4. Insure that he has a full understanding of how to plan, organize, coordinate, and, even more especially, *control*. Your own
controls will be ineffective from the standpoint of "stretch" if
his are weak.

5. Give him plenty of trust and respect.

These five principles are direct, unlarded—and efficacious. I
have seen whole treatises on delegation that covered up to 275
pages. Yet, if all the requirements of the motivational climate are
met and appropriate use is made of completed staff work (Chapter
7), the delegation process needn't be complex or abortive but should
result in the application of hitherto untapped managerial talent to
the affairs of the business. Within this framework, moreover, the de-
centralization of large divisional operations becomes possible.

Accountability Is Common Sense

The executive job may be shown diagrammatically as follows:

Responsibility			*Authority*			*Accountability*	
	⎧ People			⎧ People		People ⎫	
Plan	⎪ Money			⎪ Money		Money ⎪	
Organize	⎨ Materials	Execute	⎨ Materials	Control	Materials ⎬	Results
Coordinate	⎪ Time			⎪ Time		Time ⎪	
	⎩ Space			⎩ Space		Space ⎭	

Responsibility is the obligation of a person to carry out the assignments and functions given him by a person or persons of higher authority. *Authority* is the right to demand and expect, to issue requests which must be followed. Authority may be broken down into
line and *staff* authority, or classified as *democratic* and *autocratic* authority.

The use of authority is an effective indicator of the nature of the
person employing it. To gain compliance with his wishes, the weak
executive will often rely solely on his vested right to command. This
arbitrary or autocratic approach is normally caused by fear or ignorance; lack of confidence in one's ability to cope with a person or situation; the feeling that one's inadequacies may be discovered; ignorance or lack of enlightenment about the fundamentals of sound

management and of human motivation. Authority, however, should be used to clarify purpose and to specify and assure end results required by company objectives. It should never be used simply to further the personal ambitions of the executive. Authority used solely for this purpose ultimately reaches a point of diminishing returns. It exhausts one's mental, emotional, physical, and spiritual reservoirs, and then there is nothing. The tough-minded manager uses organizational rank as the last resort.

Accountability was defined in Chapter 2 as the clear understanding that a man does his job or gets out of it. This is common sense and should be readily understandable, but many conceive accountability to be some kind of policing device that rigidifies jobs and draws the battle lines. Rather, the concept of accountability as a motivational device requires a knowledge of how to transcend or cut across rigid organization lines and develop procedures in which accountability is implicit. For example, the production manager who knows he will not be held in any way accountable for customer complaints about quality is lacking a vital ingredient in his performance requirements. Too often it is the quality control man or the sales manager who must answer for complaints.

The converse is true, of course, and the sales manager must share accountability for production's ability to meet realistic delivery schedules. Accountability must never be repressive or coercive, but rather stretching and motivational.

Profitability Accounting

In recent years a new concept has come into management control, assuming several forms and names. Profit planning, profit center accounting, and profitability accounting are similar in that they emphasize the results achieved by individual key managers. Profitability accounting differs from the others in that these individual managers have a voice in the preparation of the yardsticks against which they are measured. It embraces the primary features of profit planning; however, initiative and responsibility are placed at the lowest possible management level, usually by these procedures:

1. The marketing and sales forecast for the next year is approved by the chief executive and the chief marketing executive.
2. Individual managers plan their operations in line with company objectives and anticipated volume.

3. Ordinarily the controller is responsible for coordinating these individual plans. Necessary changes are of course discussed with each manager. It is vital that each understand how his department fits into the total and how the total affects his operation.
4. The final plans are approved by the chief executive. Each individual plan then becomes the yardstick of the manager's performance.

In profitability accounting, the accounting department's reports are designed for the benefit of the individual operating managers. They can take whatever form the people concerned wish, but they will usually consist of the plan for the period covered, the actual results, and the reasons for any variance. These reports have become highly personalized; hardly any two firms will have similar forms.

Most companies have found the effect of profitability accounting to be so sweeping that three years is the normal time required to assimilate it throughout the organization. Customarily, the first year envisions only a few large profit centers and plans. A usual second-year plan contemplates additional profit centers at a lower level; and, of course, with more profit centers, more managers participate in the planning and in the reporting of results. By the third year companies have generally progressed down to their day-to-day managers.

An agricultural processing firm adopted profitability accounting first for its regions, then for its districts, and finally for individual truck gathering routes. To do this required several decisions regarding internal reporting and the prices of material transferred from one area of accountability to another. The resulting analysis of regions, districts, and routes led to a change of operations valued by management at $500,000 per year.

The benefits of profitability accounting, in fact, are several. As opposed to conventional budget planning it will—

1. Aid in the selection of better projects. The individual managers are encouraged to think in terms of profit as being primary.
2. Eliminate the question of whether budgeted funds are to be expended when they are in excess of need.

Still greater advantages, moreover, lie in profitability accounting's effect on management personnel. The emphasis upon results—of a manager's own plan—is an integral part of the motivational climate. For one thing, the process of planning an acceptable profit for his operation is a real growth experience for most departmental managers. And, by reviewing these plans, top management has the assurance that solid thinking is being done. If dynamic, realistic plans do not materialize, the manager must improve his planning skills.

Even more importantly, the regular reports of what happened to "his plan" show each manager what he should be able to do. An able, motivated person can produce better plans and bigger profits when he knows his past successes and errors. And this same record of successes and errors, plus the improvement of this record, forms one real basis for the manager's salary. Increasingly, the tough-minded, fully actualized organization will realize that planning is not a staff "plus" or just something that can "improve" the organization. Rather, it (planning) is innate, intrinsic, indivisible, with and to logical organizational operation.

7   *We spend most of our lives doing things. The problem is to make sure*
these "things" will yield their maximum value to ourselves or to others.

Motivate Your People

Until recently, in the world of modern business, it was un-
fashionable to reveal a strong desire for greater personal fulfillment.
Talking and writing about dollars, equipment, memos, and charts
have often been an escape from the stark realization that business
enterprises—

Were established in response to human feelings.
Exist to satisfy human feelings.
Will be dynamic or static because of human feelings.
Will succeed or fail because of human feelings.
Are of, by, about, and for *people.*

How can this be so in the face of all that has been said and done,
in recent years, in the name of "human relations"? For one thing, it
is widely felt at present that human relations—certainly in its extreme manifestations—has been a failure so far as motivating employee performance is concerned. Moreover, while conceding the
possible value of counseling an office worker, say, whose indifference may be creating problems, many executives labor under the
delusion that recognizing the importance of one's own feelings or,
worse, discussing those of fellow managers (as they may affect job

performance) is soft or unbusinesslike. This is absolutely wrong! American business is currently overlooking its greatest productive ace in the hole by this attitude. *Literally millions of people are leaving their jobs every evening with much of their energy and productivity still unused. They throw themselves into bowling, Little League baseball, and other activities with a kind of enthusiasm and identification that management has not even tapped.*

The task is to bring this unused energy and enthusiasm to bear on the job. This is discussed further in Chapter 21, "Tough-Minded MBO—a Living System of Human Dynamics."

Basic Needs and Personal Goals

We all have aspirations and yearnings. You must know yours— your people must know theirs. What, in other words, do we want from life? Why?

A lot of money?
Two cars and a fine house?
Social prestige?
Well-adjusted, responsible children?
Early retirement and travel?
A feeling of service?
Good health?
Power?

Some of these goals are worthwhile; some are meaningless and shallow. Whatever they are, most people have never refined or sharpened them. But their existence in the least of us is basic, because one useful way to fulfill our needs for recognition, opportunity, belonging, and security is to *get something done.* And, since we spend most of our lives doing things, it behooves us to make sure these "things" will yield their maximum value, either to ourselves or to others—in this case, the organization.

Here is a partial listing of employees' basic needs. Ways in which management can help follow.

Recognition
Opportunity
Belonging
Security
Significance

	Technique, Tool, or Device		Technique, Tool, or Device
Recognition	Raises	Security	Pensions
	Titles		Contracts
	Name plates		Stock purchase plans
	Service pins		Deferred compensation
Opportunity	Promotions	Significance	Clear system
	Transfers		of expectations
	Suggestion systems		
Belonging	Management clubs		
	Social clubs		
	Key to the washroom		
	Executive lunchroom		

These are only a few of the many devices on which companies today are staking their hopes for increasing job satisfaction and productivity among their people. But have these devices met the test? Far from it! They are based, too often, on the assumption that people want something for nothing, and this simply isn't true of the vast majority of employees. People approach their optimum motivation only when they see a realistic blending of personal, departmental, and company goals.

A number of less subtle approaches to the productivity problem have also been tried and found wanting. The traditional "boss," for example, uses bluster and threats to create fear. (The tough-minded leader, in contrast, creates confidence.) He drives, pulls rank, relies on authority, assumes an air of aloofness and superiority. He says "I" where the leader says "we." In short, bossism makes work drudgery while a leader makes it interesting.

For those who prefer to lead, I offer 22 specific suggestions. They are no more and no less than techniques of good management, and most of them have already been mentioned—or at least implied—in these pages.

1. Let each worker know where he stands; do not fail to discuss individual performance periodically.
2. Give credit where credit is due—commensurate with accomplishments.
3. Inform workers of changes in advance. Informed workers are more effective.
4. Let workers participate in plans and decisions affecting them.

5. Gain your workers' confidence; earn their loyalty and trust.
6. Know all your workers personally. Find out their interests, habits, and touchy points and capitalize on your knowledge of them.
7. Listen to your subordinates' proposals—they have good ideas too.
8. If a person's behavior is unusual for him, find out why. There's always a reason.
9. Try to make your wishes known by suggestion or request, whenever possible. People generally don't like to be pushed.
10. Explain the *why* of things that are to be done. Workers do a better job then.
11. When you make a mistake, admit it and apologize. Others will resent your blaming someone else.
12. Show workers the importance of every job, thus satisfying the need for security.
13. Criticize constructively; give reasons for your criticisms and suggest ways in which performance can be improved.
14. Precede criticisms with mention of a person's good points; show him you are trying to help him.
15. Do as you would have your people do. The supervisor sets the style.
16. Be consistent in your actions; let your workers be in no doubt as to what is expected of them.
17. Take every opportunity to demonstrate pride in the group. This will bring out the best in them.
18. If one person gripes, find out his grievance. One person's gripe may be the gripe of many.
19. Settle every grievance if at all possible; otherwise the whole group will be affected.
20. Set short- and long-range goals by which people can measure their progress.
21. Back up your workers. Authority must accompany responsibility.
22. Be vulnerable. The invulnerable, defensive manager not only quits growing—he begins to die. He "exists" behind his defenses.

Communication—Shared Meaning–Shared Understanding

"Communications" is a word that has been beaten to a point where it lacks almost all meaning. This is largely because so much has been said about it and so little accomplished. Yet not only is the need for good communications still real, but its absence is one of the greatest problems in business today—perhaps *the* greatest. Some good texts have been written, but, ironically, most have failed to communicate properly.

The acid test of communications is simply whether or not learning occurs as a result of the device or process. I recall spending three hours with the president and vice president of a large company discussing the implementation of the motivational climate. At the end of the three hours, the vice president said: "This is just the reverse of what we want. We don't want a bunch of gray-flannel-suit conformists—we have too damned many already." One of the essentials of the motivational climate is, of course, the development of individuals—with courage, guts, and a taste for innovation. But the point is, *I* had failed to make this clear. It was not the vice president's fault at all.

Why do I say communications are still arid? Tune in on luncheon conversations, shop conversations, committee and board-room conversations, and you hear countless exchanges which take the following direction:

- "I talked to Marian in the hall, and she *told* me she understood, but your report said . . ."
- "I sent him a memorandum; he *ought* to know."
- "I expressly understood you to say . . ."
- "As I see it, Bill, you think we aren't handling grievances properly."
- "No! That's the opposite of what I meant to say!"
- "I *assumed* you fellows had the picture. Why didn't you ask questions if you didn't understand?"

These are only a few of literally thousands of confused, costly, ulcer-producing communications mix-ups that are occurring every day in thousands of companies. (It is significant that almost the sole basis for situation comedy is lack of communication.) They are occurring in spite of a really elaborate array of communications tools and gadgets. Examples? Open houses, bulletin boards, annual reports, contests, house organs, speech classes, newsletters mailed to the home, plant tours, meetings of all kinds, recruitment manuals, attitude surveys, clubs, committees, films and other visual aids. Not to mention display posters, memos and reports, charts and graphs, em-

ployee handbooks, policy and procedure manuals, grievance procedures, community activities, reading racks, suggestion systems, on-
the-job counseling, organization charts, rumor clinics, question
boxes, pay-envelope inserts, and press, radio, and television releases.

Many of these tools are excellent for achieving specific objectives.
For instance, scheduling a series of frank discussion sessions with
union personnel after contract negotiation can have meaningful and
enlightening results. And house organs can be useful for entertainment and prestige purposes and sometimes will induce real learning.

As we have said, however, these approaches to the communications problem are too often built around that fundamental
fallacy: Employees will be stirred to high morale and productivity if
they just know what the company is doing; in other words, the mere
act of informing them accomplishes motivation. Yet some very igno-
rant people have spent a lifetime in close proximity to lots of knowledge but have learned little. The stenographer in the purchasing
department who views the job simply as doing what the boss says to
do is not likely to change any basic attitudes if an insert in the pay
envelope tells about an increase in profit over last year. Nor is the
lure of easy money through the suggestion system likely to stimulate
real innovation in such a person if—and this is frequently the case—
he or she has no idea why the purchasing department exists.

It is easy, of course, to point the finger at currently popular techniques and say what is wrong with them. On the contrary, much
good is being accomplished by many of these communications devices. What, then, is needed over and beyond them?

Good management often consists of reducing the complex to the
simple, rather than vice-versa. Further, cohesive, coordinated use of
the six queries by every person in the company is one of the most realistic ways to achieve a climate conducive to good communications.
Here, vastly oversimplified, is a pattern of approach that can be truly
meaningful when applied at every organizational level from the top
down: board of directors, president, division managers or vice presidents, department managers, section supervisors, workers:

What?	The requirements	
Where?	Where from? Where to?	*People*
When?	Past, present, future	*Money*
Who?	The person(s) involved	*Materials*
How?	Methods, techniques, tools	*Time*
Why?	Company, plan, actions	*Space*

The performance-conditioning questions to be asked under each heading are obvious. And even the rank-and-file worker can be encouraged to ask himself, for example,

> *What,* exactly, is this report I type every month?
> *Where* in the company is it sent?
> *When* is it due?
> *Who* uses it?
> *How* could I improve its readability or get it out more quickly?
> *Why* is this my responsibility and not someone else's?

Or, in a more personal vein,

> *What* is my department's real purpose?
> *Where* does my particular job fit in?
> *When* can I expect to be promoted?
> *Who* can help me prepare myself for possible advancement?
> *How* am I to know whether I am making satisfactory progress?
> *Why* should I stay with this company instead of trying my luck
>   with another?

Formidable, you say? How can we do all this and get the work out too? But this *is* getting the job done. You, the top executive, are paying for this sort of self-questioning whether you are getting it or not.

Another logical query is this: Can such an approach be used without the structured communications devices mentioned previously? The answer is that many of these devices *should* be utilized—but within an orderly, understandable framework and with a view to achieving the motivational climate throughout the company. Otherwise they will become a hodgepodge of uncoordinated activities.

The Role of the Individual Manager

So much for the fundamentals of a total environment which will encourage sound communications. What about the functional role of the individual manager?

The basic rules here are: (1) Know yourself; and (2) know how to listen. Unless you develop a clear idea of what you stand for and believe confidently that what you stand for is worthwhile, you may become a scared, uncertain person who finds it expedient to resort to defensive attitudes and protective practices. You will probably be a buck passer and a finger pointer. Afraid to look at yourself squarely, you will constantly maintain a smoke screen of big talk and little accomplishment.

A deep, abiding belief in yourself is essential if you are to hear people out when what they are saying may not be pleasant to you. Take the newly hired vice president of operations who was advised by many of her fellow managers that things were in a mess. Back stabbing was rife, morale low. The vice president listened carefully to all sides and, in addition, had an objective attitude survey carried out. Then, and only then, did he begin to take action. There had been pressure and impatience; he had been expected to react immediately to each negative tale of woe; but, where a lesser person might have been stampeded, he was tough-minded.

Listening, in short, is a real art. It takes much intestinal stamina at times, but it can pay off handsomely. The tough-minded executive finds it much easier to draw out both the good and the bad from others than does his soft-minded colleagues. Above all, he sets an example by adhering in word and deed to this important "Batten's law" of communication:

When the communicatee does not understand exactly what the communicator intended, the responsibility remains that of the communicator.

This has far-reaching ramifications. Amazing changes can occur in companies and departments where this law prevails.

Before	*After*
"You don't get what I mean."	"I didn't make myself clear."
"You didn't understand me."	"Apparently I didn't communicate."
"I told you to finish that blueprint by the 25th. Didn't you get it straight?"	"I didn't get through to you about that blueprint. Let's review what happened and make sure we have no more misunderstandings."
"You simply don't get the picture."	"Let's see where this fits in with our over-all plan."

A key talent which is important here is *empathy*. It is defined in the dictionary as "the imaginative projection of one's own consciousness into that of another person." Defined more simply, it is the knack of putting yourself in the other fellow's shoes. In business, this calls for phrasing orders and requests in ways that will be understood by people with widely varying backgrounds and abilities. Empathy, in brief, is a highly desirable quality in any manager.

The Common Denominator

Is there one common denominator of motivation? For example, of success in selling? This question, asked at many management and sales clinics, has produced such answers from sales executives as better product knowledge, more calls, concentration on "the close," gifts and premiums, good controls, personal magnetism, listening devices, memorized presentations, customer "manipulation," audiovisual aids, and competition. Not at all. The one common denominator in every successful sales situation is the ability to *make the other person see the personal benefit of your product, service, or idea.* It sounds almost too simple, doesn't it?

The tough-minded executive realizes that he or she must be an excellent salesperson. Every request, order, directive, or innovation must be *sold,* regardless of her authority, or he or she won't get full mileage out of it. Contrast the production superintendent who is ordered flatly to increase productivity in his department by 15 percent with the person who realizes the benefit of such an increase to him and to the company. You have to make a subordinate see *why,* in short, or his performance may require follow-up on your part and, perhaps, the installation of a new control.

The sales manager of an advertising specialties company was vexed because sales were bogged down in a prolonged plateau. Controls were good, and he knew what all his people were doing in terms of calls made and quantities sold. A liberal incentive plan was in operation, but still the company was not getting its full share of the market. Why? In talking to individual salespeople it was found that they thought of their work as just a job. Extra effort might yield extra earnings, but they were making good money already and were relatively complacent. Then, at a series of counseling sessions, each employee was made to see:

1. What the company stood for; why one should be proud to be a part of it.
2. What additional growth and increased company earnings could mean to each one personally: promotion, prestige, authority.
3. That the employee must answer for failure to meet new com-

mitments based on share of market and other market research findings.

4. That complacency and lack of "stretch" could, in effect, make old people out of them in a hurry.

The result was a startling acceleration in sales and a happy and newly energized sales manager.

Decisions Must Be Made!

All the components of the motivational climate can be present; but, if individual purposes, decisiveness, and action are missing, the total potential may be short-changed. It is basic that people in managerial positions must know how to accumulate pertinent information, weigh and assess the facts, and decide on a course of action. Yet too many executives lack either courage or know-how in this regard; and often, in their uncertainty, they cannot bear the thought that people may be saying the boss doesn't know the answers. They are afraid to invite appropriate participation.

Without the best thinking of your subordinates, unfortunately, you are not in the best possible position to make decisions. Without their participation, moreover, and with the poor decisions and/or procrastination which often follows, you lose their respect and drain off much potential productivity.

The principle of completed staff work, long familiar to the military, plays a powerful role here. This, as we all know, calls for studying a problem and presenting a possible solution to one's superior in such a form that all he needs to do is to approve or disapprove the recommended course of action. Completed staff work is designed to wean the subordinate of relying on the superior at every stage of an assignment for advice and decision making. In return for relieving the superior of much nonessential detail, however, it "imposes a number of responsibilities on the executive making an assignment."

1. Before you assign a problem to anyone, be sure you can define the problem. There are no solutions to unknown problems. If you cannot clearly and concisely state or write the problem, you have some more brainwork to do.
2. When you discuss a problem at a staff meeting, make it plain who is carrying the ball. You're the quarterback, but the team needs to know the play.

3. Tell the ball carrier what the problem is and what you expect him to do about it. Communication by administrative osmosis seldom produces much besides confusion and frustration.

4. Contribute your experience. You're the boss because you have superior ability. Share it with your assistants. Tell them what you have learned or what you think you have learned about the problem.

5. When you give an assignment, set a target date. Giving a person an assignment without setting a target is like asking a friend to come to dinner "some evening."

6. Be accessible for legitimate progress reports. If you don't want today's answer to yesterday's problem, or yesterday's answer to today's problem, it will pay you to take an occasional reading on progress.

7. Steadfastly resist the temptation to do your staff's thinking for them. Give guidance and background information, but make them do their own thinking. Remember that it is their job to furnish proposed solutions—not problems—and that your job is to apply management intelligence to their proposed solutions. . . .

Completed staff work is no panacea. It won't solve all your problems, but it will do this:

Free you from unimportant detail;
Multiply your executive affectiveness; and
Make your organization run better.

It all boils down to this: As an executive, you can either develop a splendid set of ulcers or teach your staff to do completed staff work. It takes about the same amount of energy either way.*

When Emotion Is an Asset

The ability to make emotion an asset in a climate of motivation and productivity really separates the tough-minded manager from those who just talk a good game. We all have emotions; they are analogous to the gasoline in any engine—they make us go. If our emotions don't make us turn on our personal ignitions, nothing happens.

In our subordinates, emotions can be a tremendous help or a distinct liability. Taking advantage of them presupposes certain basic requirements:

*J. Lewis Powell, "Completed Staff Work: Key to Effective Delegation," MANAGEMENT REVIEW, June 1956, pp. 502–503.

1. You must understand that emotion has to be positive.
2. You must relate the desired response to what the subordinate can do, not what he can't do.
3. You must be motivated yourself by a desire to develop some quality or skill in the subordinate, not to restrain it.
4. You must recognize that learning implies a change in behavior, not just polite absorption of knowledge, and make the subordinate see how that change will benefit him.
5. You must understand his needs for emotional security, recognition, opportunity, and a feeling of belonging, and these must be related to the greater purpose you have in mind (that is, a sense of personal purpose must be focused on company and/or departmental goals).
6. You must exercise your powers of empathy. Don't just assume the other person knows what you mean—*make sure* he does.

When all these conditions are met, you have every right—even an obligation—to *require* performance. In summary, the words of George S. Dively, chairman of the board of the Harris Corporation, may be timely:

. . . I have found the "certain something" that the top companies appear to have, which I call "creative management," to be a combination of well-defined corporate objectives understood at all management levels, an effective sense of research in the development of new solutions and ideas, and a great skill in developing management people from both the enthusiasm and continuity viewpoints. Also, there must be a forceful leader to inspire, activate, and guide these management activities.

The effective application of these factors in a business seems to produce that high peak of efficiency resulting from policy foresight and effective administration; that tone of progressiveness resulting from cultivated imagination; and that enthusiasm, drive, and continuity of good executives which produces management leadership. The net result should be a stronger competitive position, which is the real basis for better products for customers, more attractive jobs for employees, larger dividends for shareholders, and broader public service.

. . . I strongly feel that this type of management can give us not only the greatest possible safeguard for our competitive free enterprise system but the greatest opportunity for its continuing progress. No other system in the history of the world has approached the ability of this competitive system of ours to provide for the wants and protect the rights of the people as a whole. Creative management *can* and *must* keep that system strong, and see that it evolves in line with the hopes and aspirations of the people it serves.

To determine, think about, and respond to the wants, needs, and problems of others so that they in turn help fulfill your goals—*this* is the pragmatic essence of motivation.

8

Lean, taut performance is the goal.

Control and Insure Progress

THE concept of control is currently misunderstood and misused by many executives. Reams of copy have been turned out on the subject, with the result that control has been made to sound like a truly complex set of mechanisms. In this chapter, however, I want to reduce control—its meaning, purpose, and method—to very simple terms, if only because its potential in the tough-minded environment is so great.

First of all, control may be defined as

Information provided to measure the performance of people, money, materials, time, and space in achieving predetermined objectives.

At present it is often an instrument which compresses the individual, sets arbitrary ceilings and grooves for performance, and is deeply rooted in the past and the status quo. Ideally, control should be a dynamic instrument, pulling, stretching, and challenging the potential of everyone in the company.

Control is not strictly historical; it should also be prognostic.

Where Are We Going?

If we are to conceive of control not merely as a record of the past, with the emphasis on accounting, but as a fluid instrument for gauging the present and future motivational temperature of the total company climate, we must first break our means of control down into categories.

People	Money	Materials	Time	Space
Performance appraisal	Budgets	Statistical quality control	Time study	Cost per square foot
Psychological tests	Forecasts	Visual inspection	Deadlines	Productivity per square foot
Accountability	Profit planning	Inspection instruments	Commitments	Standard procedures
Time study	Profitability accounting	Operations manuals	Forecasts	Estimates
Committees	Audits	Work measurement	Schedules	Reports
Staff meetings	Return on investment	Inventory control	Work measurement	Memoranda
Manpower inventories	Standard costs	Estimates	Reports	Ratios
Policy manuals	Policy manuals	Blueprints	Standard procedures	Charts
Organization manuals	Work measurement	Standard procedures	Memoranda	Etc.
Work measurement	Standard procedures	Reports	Ratios	
Performance requirements	Reports	Memoranda	Charts	
Standard procedures	Memoranda	Ratios	Etc.	
Reports	Ratios	Charts		
Memoranda	Charts	Etc.		
Ratios	Etc.			
Charts				
Etc.				

This partial list should serve both to enlighten and to confuse. It is enlightening to realize that so many forms of control exist in a typical business. It is confusing to try to assemble them into a purposeful, efficient order.

The chief reason for listing these devices with their obvious overlap is to show that control must not be thought of as a set of convenient buttons to push. Rather, it can be viewed first as a concept based on these premises:

Planning {
1. An organization exists only for accomplishment.
2. People work within a business only for accomplishment.
3. Resources are employed only for accomplishment.

Organizing
4. The right combination and balance of resources are needed for accomplishment.

Coordination and Execution
5. These resources must work in consonance with each other for accomplishment.

Therefore,

Control
6. The effectiveness of these foregoing steps is measured only for accomplishment.

From this conceptual view we see clearly that the prime purpose of control is to determine not *where we have been* but *where we are going*.

Each of the control devices listed should be subjected to the most penetrating scrutiny to determine whether it is lending itself directly to individual, departmental, or company accomplishment. If its value appears to be historical only, action should be taken according to the following sequence:

Eliminate it altogether; *or*
Combine its elements with a better control device; *or*
Rearrange them to meet necessary criteria; *or*
Simplify the device as applicable.

Above all, beware of gray areas. I have seen many instances of unnecessary friction between boss and subordinate because of uncertainties in interpersonal control.

The general manager of a grain-processing company was having a lot of trouble with the production superintendent. "I have given definite instructions time and again, but things never really get wrapped up." Investigation showed that the general manager's orders and requests were largely limited to *what* was to be done—he seldom specified *when*. Once he began to lay out firm, clear control dates and quantities for the superintendent, the situation improved considerably. It was only, however, after company and departmental objectives had been developed and communicated to the superintendent, along with the results required of the position, that real harmony and productivity were brought about.

Blind Dedication Can Be Costly

Oftentimes the very excellence of a person's work is at cross purposes with the company's goals if those goals are not understood.

A medium-size manufacturer of consumer and gift items was faring badly with its competition. Profits had dropped, and the president decided that profit planning was the answer. A new controller was hired and given wide latitude in installing a "profit plan." Unfortunately, the controller didn't know the real difference between a budget and a profit plan. Accordingly, he introduced tight budgetary control; and, exercising the authority that had freely been given, created an environment that tended to reflect unfavorably on any executive who exceeded budget. Cost reduction and cost control became principal performance criteria, and the company's competitive position got worse rapidly.

It was eventually discovered that what the company needed most was new competitive products, much over-all innovation. Efforts in this direction had withered fast under the cost controls and strict budgeting concepts introduced by the new controller, since insufficient money was appropriated for research, for methods improvement, and for other activities necessary to innovation. Here was a case where an excellent financial executive was apparently carrying out the wishes of the superior yet precipitating the company into greater difficulties than before. What does the tough-minded manager do to avoid this? He checks back to see that—

1. Over-all objectives are sound.
2. All key personnel understand them.
3. The end results required of each major function are set up in the way most conducive to accomplishing these objectives.
4. Communication is effective—and reciprocal.
5. Other components of the motivational climate are present.

Tough-minded management also recognizes that while control should not stifle or compress people, it must be closely related to discipline and guidance. To assume that the inexperienced employee is completely capable of finding his way in a foggy, permissive company environment is to assume that a child will automatically absorb and understand all the laws, customs, and mores of the society we live in.

Discipline—particularly self-discipline—is wholesome and essential, provided that it is exercised in the direction of positive accomplishment. The tough mind is a disciplined mind, not bound by rigid parameters but trained and drilled in the impatient search for further growth, further contributions, and certainly further achievements. Enlightened purpose, rather than blind dedication, is the thing.

More Paper

On occasion, I have asked a president or major division head what kind of control he has. The response often is to pull some statistical reports or charts out of a desk drawer and display them proudly. But is this really control? Or is it self-delusion? Elaborate paper controls may exist in an organization, yet interviews with second- and third-level people will bring to light low morale, low productivity, buck passing, politics, and other problems arising from frustration and inadequate motivation.

The net result of control, then, too often is simply to tell management what is wrong from a purely quantitative standpoint, or to indicate what *can't* be done. To overcome this tendency, everyone in the organization must be encouraged, through proper communications techniques, to view paper as having only one purpose: to get something done. If it is accomplishing nothing and will accomplish nothing, junk it.

Once more, it is important that the guiding philosophy come from the top. This kind of control may be intangible, but it is *real*. It is effective because people from the top down perform because they want to—with purpose, direction, and desire. Attempting to control the progress of a company through the manipulation of data is like building a house with cards. The substance—people, reactions—just isn't there, and you often wind up controlling only your own emotions.

Some Kind of Feedback

It is axiomatic that feedback must occur both as a result and as a prerequisite of an action. For instance, if you issue a lengthy and detailed order to a subordinate and he does not seek to have it clarified in any respect, it is often safe to assume that either he doesn't know enough to ask questions or you are unusually articulate. Since you can't always rely on your skill as a communicator, it is well to ask for feedback. This means, simply, that you request the subordinate to give you back the essence of what you have said so that you may verify that it is understood, or modify and amplify your instructions to insure understanding.

We are frequently told that this method is too elementary to use on other members of management or on technical people, that it insults their intelligence. In view of the sad mistakes that result from faulty communication, this just isn't so. Communication control must be built into the motivational climate. Where all employees realize their full responsibility in the communication process, feedback is a normal and natural thing.

Feedback to insure the effective launching of a project, we have seen, is important. It is even more important when used as a method of measuring final results. In general, we have three different kinds of feedback:

1. Oral feedback of requests, orders, and the like.
2. Paper documents: reports, charts, other data.
3. Electronic or mechanical forms of feedback, such as EDP.

Profitability accounting, for instance, may require all three kinds of feedback during installation and for evaluation purposes as well. Thus performance counseling may call for oral feedback in the interview, will undoubtedly make use of a performance scale and appraisal forms, and will almost certainly be based on results as shown by electronically tabulated reports. All these various types of control, in the final analysis, are pieces in the total mosaic—the motivational climate. All are for, by, and about people.

To Measure Performance

In the past few years it has become the mark of a management pundit to repeat often and sagely: "We must measure performance." This is a flawless, laudable, and impeccable statement, but few people really know how to do it. Return on investment has been widely heralded as one over-all measure of top executive performance and, properly administered (see Chapter 3), it can be most helpful. But what about measuring the effectiveness of executives and managers at successively lower company levels? The following program can be truly meaningful and is still relatively unique:

1. A performance standards sheet is prepared for each of several factors. For example:
    Ratio of direct to indirect labor.
    Scrap loss.
    Turnover.
    Absenteeism.
    Safety (lost time, workmen's compensation, law suits, etc.).
    Consumer complaints.
    Vendor complaints.
    Ratio of net profit to sales.
    Ratio of selling expense to sales volume.
2. A set of these sheets, or an appropriate master sheet, is given to each executive.
3. Each executive is counseled on how to get his department in order. This means establishing a taut ship, with emphasis on such matters as organization, administration, costs, personal relations, operating improvements, and planning for the future.
4. Each person then makes commitments for each factor by month, quarter, or year as applicable.
5. Extenuating circumstances are worked out in advance and agreed upon. Thus they become relatively inflexible.
6. You, the top executive, maintain a record of all commitments in a concise, neat book (it might be labeled "Administrative Controls") and keep your eye on them.
7. Each month, or as often as agreed upon, your subordinates furnish activity reports which provide information on their progress toward meeting commitments and any other data which may be desirable.
8. These periodic results-oriented progress reports are regularly reviewed, offering you a valuable opportunity for objective appraisal and systematic development.

Such a program provides both push and pull through (*a*) disciplinary action (push) if commitments are not met, which may mean transfer, demotion, dismissal, or perhaps just additional training if it seems likely to pay off; and (b) reward for exceeding commitments (pull) in terms of raises, promotions, reassignments, and so on.

This is, of course, only a skeletal outline of a procedure which has many potential advantages over traditional activity-oriented management. Planning skills must be developed by everyone concerned, and a climate is established in which the taut ship prevails and the development of efficient subordinates is encouraged. Rewards are directly related to actual achievements. In addition, the system requires interdepartmental cooperation and coordination; and, since the end-result measurements in use are so strongly dependent on an integrated team effort, much internal politicking is eliminated.

Follow-up Can Make or Break You

The primary use of control in the motivational climate, as we have noted, is to achieve maximum productivity of people and of other company resources. Control, in other words, should be a catalyst. What does the tough-minded administrator do, however, when faced with poor performance and variance from required results in spite of his control procedures? And this can happen from time to time even in the well-ordered environment we have described. It can happen because the individual executive is composed of a mass of variables which are seldom fully understood even by the individual himself.

If, then, faulty performance occurs, the tough-minded manager once again reviews his objectives to insure their soundness and makes certain that subordinates understand them. Once again he reviews the attributes of each of his employees: Is each familiar with his or her field in general? Has he kept up to date in job know-how? Will he accept responsibility? (Have responsibility and authority been properly delegated to him?) What is his attitude toward the company and his place in it? Further, the superior examines each of his subordinates' relations with others (ability to supervise and motivate, sense of teamwork, ease of self-expression); his basic character (intelligence, integrity, drive, perseverance, ambition, courage, cooperation, judgment, emotional maturity). Are there clearly defined personal values? Is his thinking positive rather than negative?

The tough-minded manager insures again that departmental and company goals are identified with personal goals, and that the purpose and nature of the controls established are understood. He makes a new effort to focus on people's strengths instead of their weaknesses. In each employee's case, he sets a time limit for improvement and spells out the action to be taken if that improvement does not occur. Accountability must be fact—not fiction.

An often-told story goes this way: An employee was told by his superior to dig a hole. As soon as the hole was dug, he was told to fill it up. Then he was instructed to dig a second hole and to fill it up too. After his third hole he declared, "I quit—this is silly." The supervisor finally explained that he was trying to locate an old pipeline. "Why didn't you tell me?" demanded the employee. "I was stationed here during the war when this was a fort, and I helped lay that pipeline." He promptly took the boss to the exact spot in question.

Ridiculous? Once in a million? Not at all! This kind of thing is going on all over the country with infinite variations. So, if performance falters, make sure you get the complete *why*.

Controls Must Pay for Themselves

Just as there is no reason for a person to be on a payroll if he fails to pay his way, so it is with controls. Some people tend to become chart-happy. Others get ecstatic over statistics.

The expanding role of big government has done much to make management more difficult; and, regrettably, bureaucracy has spawned a conglomerate of reports and apparently useless activity in too many organizations. Businesspeople often take sly swipes at government inefficiency and red tape. But I have noticed an ever greater amount of internal red tape and "controls" in companies managed by some of these people.

I remember one firm in particular where a messy situation existed. The systems and procedures manager was fond of weighty and verbose standard practice instructions. Over a period of years, numerous operating executives in subsidiary plants resigned— usually for reasons which were of two sorts: either flawless and understandable or quite obscure. Eventually, though, a plant manager wrote the president of the company stating that the volume of home office procedures was strangling him to the point where he felt he must soon resign—and that this, further, was why other good people had left. Subsequent research showed that he was right, and the systems and procedures department came in for some close scrutiny.

Eighty percent of the SOP's were junked, and a new vitality zipped through the company.

Lesson: Make controls pay for themselves.

In essence, *real* control consists of *people* who know *what* is to be done, *when* it must be done, *where* it must be done, *who* must be involved and committed, *how* it can be done, and, above all, *why* it must be done. Charts, graphs, and other mechanistic tools are only *manifestations* of real control.

9   *I will live my life on the cutting edge. I will confront my*
possibilities.

Stressing Positives for Tough-Minded Results

I HAVE seen many big people who are small in size. They have a well-developed zest and hunger for living, for creating, for building, and for giving.

In order to encourage such growth, to expand the personalities, talents, and productivity of those around you, you must continue to expand your own personality, talents, and productivity. Your resources here are not financial but consist of values, attitudes, aptitudes, and abilities.

American business needs big people as it never has before. Today's kaleidoscopic world happenings require *adaptable* people, *positive* attitudes.

The Real Challenge

In his book *The Man in Management,*[1] Lynde Steckle has headed a chapter "Why Stress Positives?" and has proceeded to supply some sound answers. The tough-minded executive should be impatient

[1] Lynde Steckle, *The Man in Management,* Harper & Row (1958).

for a deep understanding of "positive thinking." Is it no more than a catch-phrase at which the more sophisticated of us snicker? What specific implications does it have for management?

First, let me quote from the writings of Saul W. Gellerman:

> It seems to me that the greatest challenge facing management today is to meet the need for a feeling of accomplishment and significance in people's work. Our great need now is for working atmospheres in which latent creativity, deftness, or just plain love of hard work can blossom forth. Boredom is not so much a problem in itself as it is a symptom of management's newest frontier—*maximizing the achievement potential of its people*.

> There are many reasons why this challenge should be taken up, some of which are more worthy than others. Unleashing the full achievement power of individuals and groups would, of course, give an enormous boost to the very process we have already carried so far forward: making things for people to use, admire and luxuriate in. But that is not where the real challenge lies—nor, indeed, does it lie in some vaguely humanitarian opportunity to make people happier on the job. The basic reason why management should undertake to maximize its people's chances to achieve all they can is simply this: it is the most difficult possible challenge to management's own ability to manage. It is management's opportunity to develop its *own* skills and potentialities to their highest levels.[2]

This is positive thinking and practice on the firing line of business. Let's see it, then, as a type of thing which is difficult for many, which is challenging, but which can pay enormous dividends in accomplishment and satisfaction.

I have stated previously that in many organizations you can literally feel the climate that exists. To this I would add, with conviction, the following statement: It is often possible to form a pretty accurate idea of the profit and loss position of a company solely on the basis of the bigness of the person at the helm. When she has successfully implanted the idea among her people that they are all there to get something done, that "the difficult we do today—the impossible only takes a little longer," the profit and loss statement is usually good.

The Little Person

For several years businesspeople of all kinds have been undergoing an agonizing appraisal of themselves, their companies, and the

---

[2] Saul W. Gellerman, *People, Problems, and Profits,* McGraw-Hill Book Company (1960), p. 245.

business community in general. Price fixing has received the most publicity, but there have been other charges of exploitation and greed. These have resulted in charges, countercharges, and much defensive anxiety. William H. Whyte, Jr., for one, takes a scathing look at the many attempts on the part of business men to "carry their message to the people."[3]

It is a basic manifesto of this book that the head of each organization must start such therapeutic action in his own backyard. Many recent criticisms have not been justified, but many have been. This all ties in very fundamentally with the presence or lack of positive attitudes. The big person takes a hard look at himself and his business and resolves to set an example of leadership and positive action for his own people and the industry as a whole. An outstanding example of positive leadership is James Lincoln of the Lincoln Electric Company. He took positive steps to relate the personal needs and goals of his employees to the objectives of the company. The emphasis was not on self-aggrandizement, or something for nothing, but rather on greater returns for greater productivity.

What, in contrast, are the symptoms of the "little" person?

1. He is wrapped up in himself and his own interests.
2. He has many fears—for example, that people will take advantage of him.
3. He makes the simple seem complex—so it usually is.
4. He thinks of the easy as difficult and the difficult as impossible. Again, they usually are.
5. He thinks in terms of actions rather than end results.
6. He accepts others' ideas with reluctance, if at all. When he does, he may represent them as his own.
7. He often wants something for nothing.
8. He is critical of others' weaknesses and seldom acknowledges their strengths.
9. He lacks a real and abiding faith in himself or in anyone else.
10. He is defensive and seeks invulnerability.

I am referring, of course, not only to men who are obviously cringing, fawning, and obsequious, but to many so-called "tough" people. Here again, the distinction must be sharply etched between the belligerent, unjustly demanding executive and the one who is really tough-minded. The tough-minded executive is sure enough of himself that he does not require the trappings and symbols of au-

---

[3] William H. Whyte, Jr., *Is Anybody Listening?* Simon and Schuster, New York, (1952).

thority. How authority is used determines whether or not he is a big person.

Defense Mechanisms

It is a common and normal human tendency to think of many actions by the little—and sometimes selfish and vindictive—person as deliberate. This is true to the extent that a person's knowledge affects his interpretation of right and wrong. But often a scared or insecure executive or worker does things that he not only knows are wrong but does not even wish to do. What psychologists call "defense mechanisms" come into play.

Our goal here is for operating insight only, rather than an involved clinical treatment. However, some defense mechanisms in the organizational situation include:

1. Rationalization—"I didn't want it anyway." This mechanism often takes over almost unconsciously to protect a person from emotional stress. Executives of all ages who cannot face up to something often take refuge in the feeling that what happened wasn't so bad after all. This can be healthy or unhealthy, depending on the man and the circumstances.

2. Compensation—"I'll show them this is *one* thing I'm *really* good at." This involves trying extra hard for some form of achievement to make up for a disappointment. We see many people driven by forces they don't understand in an unceasing quest for a particular kind of success. Sometimes this involves trampling on one's best friends.

3. Projection—"I may have made the mistake, but you caused it." We find a lot of people conveniently attaching the blame for their mistakes to someone else. Many who make this a habit genuinely feel they are highly moral and even tough-minded.

4. Daydreaming—"Pie in the sky"; "cross the chasm without building a bridge"; "I'll do it *mañana*." There are splendid, gregarious "nice people" who can talk up a storm but who seldom get anything *done*. They have not learned the necessity for facing up to situations, developing controls for themselves, and ramming through a real achievement.

These few defense mechanisms will help the tough-minded manager toward a better understanding of "bastardly" actions on the part of others. It should be truly exciting for the really big person to encourage subordinates to overcome "little person" tendencies, to discover new strengths, to shape up and grow.

Sarcasm—Expedient of the Weak

The habitual use of brittle, witty sarcasm, of "perfect squelches," has no place in the motivational climate. The manager who feels impelled to meet situations in this way is usually taking a path that requires no courage.

Yet cruelty of this sort is appallingly common in human relationships of all kinds today; and business, unfortunately, is no exception. Tough-minded administrators must ask themselves, "What can possibly be gained by squelching a person sarcastically other than an unrealistic, momentary feeling of power?" Let's label sarcasm for what it is—a gutless expedient of the weak personality.

It takes much more courage to give the other person a bit of counsel which helps to develop her in some way. Wholesome humor and facetious remarks can often lighten and stimulate a grim meeting. Humor, in fact, is important, but the question should always be asked, "Will it do something *for* him or *to* him?" Sarcasm can be nourished only by relating to weaknesses. And this the tough-minded manager shuns.

Cynicism—Corrosive Refuge

A cynic is defined by the dictionary as ". . . one who believes that human conduct is motivated only by self-interest." The spectacle of the cynic is a sorry one. He is a little person, and many times the cynical individual is incapable of seeing the virtues and abilities that other people have.

A dyed-in-the-wool cynic in the midst of an otherwise healthy department can have far-reaching effects. He is often the "abominable no man" referred to earlier. But I have seen instances where such a worker makes a marked change for the better when exposed to the outgoing results-oriented climate made possible by tough-minded management. She must be all but pulled out of herself; if, instead, she is allowed to retire within the sometimes comfortable refuge of self-preoccupation, more than likely she ends up no happier.

Fear Can Kill

Fear is a fog hovering over the world, soaking in and dampening us as we move through life. And it is all so unnecessary! This is not to say that fear is easily eradicated, but there are definite principles and guideposts which will point the way if people will only apply them. To discuss tough-minded performance in the competitive business world without treating fear would be to dodge a vital issue.

In speeches and lectures I have often mentioned fear of subordinates as a cause of procrastination, indecision, and anxiety. This is sometimes challenged. "What kind of person would fear subordinates," someone asks, "when you can easily fire them?" It's not this simple. Sometimes you fear a subordinate because of the very excellence of his work. You feel guilty because (you think) he highlights your own inadequacies.

The purchasing director of a major company worried so much about her up-and-coming assistant that she was close to a nervous breakdown. Investigation revealed that the concern was principally traceable, not to anything the subordinate had said or done, but to the fact that she had a master's degree while the purchasing director didn't even have a bachelor's degree. Yet the subordinate had no designs on the boss's job but was concentrating on a widely different path of promotion. The two had not communicated effectively.

In another case, the youthful manager of a small cooperative was so frozen by indecision and fear of what veteran subordinates would say that he apparently was watching earnings go down and doing nothing about it. He felt that the old-timers would label whatever he did as "newfangled" and impractical. Actually, the old-time employees had looked forward eagerly to seeing what new blood and young ideas could contribute. But, again, they had not communicated effectively.

Fears can multiply rapidly if we let them. But fears are destructive largely because of the ignorance of the people involved—and this statement in no way excludes highly educated people. Vast numbers of people have not had the opportunity to discover what the motivational climate can accomplish, and the positive approach is one of its most important components.

People develop fears for more reasons than we can identify here, but the chief reasons in a business environment include lack of self-understanding; lack of purpose, direction, and understanding of one's role; failure to understand why other people do as they do (e.g., the defense mechanisms); failure to recognize goals or objectives, either of one's self or of the company; concentration on weaknesses instead of strengths; lack of knowledge about the cause of one's fear; and so on.

I recently dined in one of the best-known restaurants in Chicago. The place was packed with business people of all kinds, with particular emphasis on smart dressers between 25 and 45. The "job talk" I overheard began to intrigue me as the crowd at the bar and the people at nearby tables spoke more and more freely. I stayed for two hours, just listening. The net result of all these conversations was many remarks by voluble and apparently ambitious people about what was wrong with companies, jobs, and individuals, and what people were doing to each other, but not one remark about what should be done to improve the situation.

This is a serious commentary on much that is happening these days. Here were people in effect asking for trouble, for doubts and fears. One leaves sessions of this kind with new knowledge, but not the kind that is good for one. The tough-minded top executive will take steps to help his people to find purpose, direction, and goals and will seek to blend these with the purposes of the organization. To do less is to cultivate the negative sort of thinking that is already too prevalent. There is much positiveness lying dormant in people. It must be released and directed, or a weak, muddled business community will continue to evolve.

Make Tension an Asset

If the real nature of tough-minded management is not understood, it can appear to be the kind of thing that causes tensions. This is not true. Rather, the little person described earlier in this chapter is well on his way toward a way of life calculated to produce undesirable tensions and anxieties. Think only of yourself, of immediate gain, of how to exploit your fellow workers, and you invite destruction. This is not pollyanna thinking, not a sweet nostrum, but demonstrated fact. The tensions which harm you are those caused by an undue concern with self.

Public speakers often experience tensions which can be either exhilarating or fatiguing. The speaker who is a "pro" is the one whose mind is on the audience and its growth or entertainment rather than on self. The real pro is leaning into the audience with a reaching mind and is thinking, "What is the one best way to phrase what I have to say so that maximum understanding is achieved?" Such a person can easily talk for four and even eight hours without notice-able fatigue.

On the other hand, the beginner—or the person who is still an amateur after 80 speeches—worries and asks painful questions as he gets ready to talk: "Just how formidable is this audience? What will these people think of me? Will they be bored or hostile?" Tensions develop which wear him down, and usually he is emotionally drained at the end of 30 minutes.

This same principle applies to people's daily work and life. We have all known people who seem to be tireless; we marvel at their energy and wonder what makes them hold up. Generally, such peo-ple are outgoing in purpose and character and are focusing on end results of a positive nature.

Suppose that sales suddenly dip 20 percent. This kind of thing can create, and has created, consternation and tension in a company. The soft-minded executive immediately seeks to fix blame, to focus only on what went wrong. The tough-minded executive is more con-cerned about what has to be done and takes action accordingly. This does not rule out fact finding and research; it simply recognizes that the only benefit in finding out what happened yesterday is to make positive things happen tomorrow.

Several years ago a number of articles appeared in newspapers and magazines about the high incidence, at top management levels, of tension-related ailments such as ulcers, heart attacks, and nervous breakdowns. This caused great concern among executives and would-be executives. Some, feeling they must achieve tranquility above all else, tried to remove all tension from their work. The result, in many cases, was a blandness and an artificial complacency which took a lot of pleasure out of life. Others, of course, benefited greatly because their self-examination revealed sources of negative tension and anxiety and they were able to take corrective steps.

The person who is organically sound and fitted by aptitude and emotional make-up for his work needs a measure of zest and enthu-siasm to do a good job. This produces a healthy form of tension, and the motivational climate contains the ingredients to make tension an asset.

Let Yourself Go

The prevalence of drawn-faced people in business is too great. Many executives with great knowledge and good intentions are currently inhibiting growth and innovation in their departments or companies simply because they themselves are inhibited as individuals.

When you are inhibited, you hold yourself back; you fail to give freely of your energy, enthusiasm, and knowledge to worthwhile, productive enterprises. You can be highly educated and thoroughly experienced and still not know how to open up and be creative, to "freewheel" and bring new ideas to life.

Here are some of the stumbling blocks to letting yourself go:

Fear—of failure, of ridicule, of superiors and subordinates.
Pressure—to conform, to bend, to meet impossible deadlines.
Timidity—reluctance to face up to challenge.
Perfectionism—the urge to do it the one best way or not at all.
Habits—repetitive actions and patterns which perpetuate themselves.
Attitudes—based on the past and the status quo.

In contrast, the entire concept of the motivational climate is calculated to provide the employee with stretch, push, identification, participation—a total environment in which associates, subordinates, and superiors put forth more effort because *everyone's doing it.*

Let's face it—even the most tough-minded person is periodically plagued by one or more of these stumbling blocks. The measure of this person, however, is what she does about it. She may react by becoming increasingly conservative and austere, by striking out at those around her, or by resorting to other defense mechanisms. She may become an alcoholic.

The tough-minded manager recognizes that few people are inhibited because they want to be. The paralysis of indecision is caused by something; he wants to get at this cause and remedy it. He wants to make sure that the environment includes, for each employee,

1. The understanding that creativity is the thing—that people will not be penalized for rocking the boat. We hear lots of pious lip service to this policy, but it is up to the responsible executive to *prove* he will back the innovator. Remember, a subordinate's idea can be curdled by only a glance or an injudicious comment from his boss. The superior, in short, must live innovation rather than just talk about it. He must exemplify that vulnerability and strength are one.

2. A thorough understanding of the nature, purpose, information requirements, and end-result requirements of his position.
3. A similarly thorough understanding of his strengths and potential which should make continued emphasis on his weaknesses unnecessary. And that he will be *expected* to do so.
4. Communication, through all appropriate media, of the fact
   that few if any of us are using our potential abilities to the
   fullest.

I once had occasion to meet with the president and executive
staff of a medium-sized Midwestern company to discuss some major
issues. During the entire hour and a half, the only persons who
spoke were the president, the vice president, and I. There were
some capable people in the group, and I knew that the final decisions reached would have been better if they had participated. But
they were inhibited, locked in, worried about self-preservation. The
president told me later that she very much wanted freewheeling participation and had tried numerous devices, such as brainstorming
and training sessions in conference leadership, to stimulate it. However, she herself was a reserved, formal, almost austere woman, and
her staff was definitely afraid of her.

A climate was needed here, not just a series of devices. An executive who wants more ideas from his organization first has to create a
feeling of safety—of freedom to fail. This will be only a laudable
statement, however, until each manager—at each level—exemplifies
sufficient openness, care, and vulnerability that subordinates know it
is a reality. The day of the impregnable, "uptight," and "superior"
executive is waning fast. What kind are *you* becoming?

10

The topnotch manager
marshals language to his aid.

Action Words
and Concepts

Peter Drucker, in his classic *The Practice of Management*,[1] makes a strong appeal for broader and deeper academic preparation for management responsibilities. The taciturn or inarticulate person, he says, has a much rougher row to hoe in aspiring to executive assignment than does his more expressive counterpart. He finds that the tools of management are increasingly becoming words and concepts. The ability to secure the cooperation of others through direct, lucid word usage was never more needed.

Overcoming Resistance to Change

Some writers, as we have seen, feel the tendency to resist change is basic to people—that it is normal and natural to form fixed ideas and practices. Here we take a different stand: that people fundamentally need and must have change, that the widespread resistance to change in business is the result of a nonmotivational climate, rooted deeply in the past and the youth of many people.

---

[1] Peter F. Drucker, *The Practice of Management,* Harper & Row (1954).

We have said that to bring about a change in basic attitudes it is necessary to—

Help the other person see the personal benefit of the change.
Establish an emotional context.
Communicate.

Skill in choosing and using combinations of words is important to the accomplishment of both steps. Facile, penetrating, incisive, crunchy words can often accomplish much more than the most elaborate charts and graphs. And the topnotch manager of tomorrow *must* marshal them to his aid, or he just won't be able to stretch and pull his people or unleash his own energies and drives into positive channels.

Wendell Johnson brings home the value of words and the urgency of their mastery in these terms:

> Whenever the stakes are precious, words must not fail us any more. The same scientific method by which we have made our means of destruction so utterly effective must be used to make our communications, and so our social organization, correspondingly efficient. In releasing the long-pent-up fury of the atom, we have created for ourselves the necessity of quickly becoming what we might have been, of designing and establishing a scientific education that will wipe out our semantic blockades which make impossible the sanity and cooperation that are now simply essential for remaining alive. We can no longer afford serious conflict, aggression, contempt, and hate. We can no longer tolerate studied confusion, cultivated distrust, and verbal irresponsibility. It is neither an academic nor a moral issue. It is a practical, down-to-earth question of survival. Uranium hangs heavy over our heads so long as we strive to preserve beliefs, loyalties and institutions that disunite us—so long as we cherish the old superstitions, prides and prejudices with which we have muddled through to the crumbling edge of blinding disintegration.[2]

Think Big but Speak Simply

Now is a time for big thinkers in all dimensions of our society! The edges of understanding need to be pushed ahead constantly. Tremendous challenges remain in marketing, transportation, au-

---

[2] Wendell Johnson, *People in Quandaries*, Harper & Row (1946), p. 482.

tomation, engineering, money management, materials management, human motivation. Yet much of the current literature continues to repeat and perpetuate the status quo.

Too often big words and big thinking are considered to be the same. This is seldom the case. The person whose mind is whirring rapidly, who is dedicated to obtaining new answers to business problems, feels no need—indeed, she doesn't have the time—to express herself with ponderous verbosity. This is not to say that the highly capable person has a limited vocabulary. The reverse is true, because one of the best ways of learning to speak simply, concisely, succinctly, is to understand so many words and word combinations that an orderly and simple kind of expression is made easy.

The point is that the person who is getting things done usually feels no real need to impress others with purely verbal accomplishments. The time-worn adage that nothing speaks more eloquently than results still needs repeating. However, we must understand that results in the pure sense almost always require the ability to make words work for us. Hence real accomplishment and innovation are seldom possible when the executive clutters his mind with fat, pontifical phrases.

It follows that the person who waxes eloquent and long-winded at the slightest opportunity is usually throwing up a smoke screen to hide a lack of real achievement. What implications does this have for tough-minded management? New breakthroughs in semantics are urgently needed. We must move beyond reinvention of the wheel.

Reports: Get to the Point

Written policies, procedures, and memoranda are important—in their place. The burgeoning growth of many businesses has made it imperative to communicate all sorts of information in this way. Written policies, for example, provide—

A clear picture of company objectives.
Assistance in delegating authority.
Over-all guidance and meaning for individual growth.
Added meaning for planning.
Stability and system.
Orientation for new employees.
Aid in management by exception.
Consistency and continuity.

Coordination and understanding; teamwork.

A means of unifying individual talents.

A means of welding programs into a *system*.

A sound statement of policy should aim at clarity, flexibility, consistency, and individuality. If well planned and articulated, it should also reflect such intangibles as the flavor, warmth, and background of the business. It is vital that it be conceived within a workable and effective climate. There have been some magnificently worded policies which failed almost completely to accomplish their purpose—usually because the document would not stand alone. Policy preparation without planning, without coordination, execution, or follow-through, is as meaningless as a military directive to take a town without troops or logistics.

A procedure is defined by George R. Terry as "a series of related tasks that make up the chronological sequence and the established way of performing the work to be accomplished."[3] Procedures are known variously as standard operating procedures, standard practice instructions, and sometimes systems. Procedures are used in all companies whether or not they are formalized and recognized as such. Moreover, *you pay for procedures—whether you have good or bad ones.*

Many companies have feared that policy and procedures manuals might rigidify their operations, that the initiative of lower echelons might be lessened along with imagination and innovation. This very thing can happen—but only when the real purposes of the guidelines are not understood, when they are poorly prepared and/or a climate of apathy exists.

The effective use of policy and procedures manuals has often been hamstrung by the writers themselves. Primary among the causes is that archaic, ponderous language sometimes called "businessese." It is replete with such phrases as these:

"Coordination shall be duly rendered. . . ."

"All items to be purchased shall be cleared and coordinated with the responsible officer. . . ."

"If sufficient facts render the matter appropriate, clearance will be rendered. . . ."

I remember a large supermarket which was taken in by the salesmanship of a smooth-talking "consultant." Three weeks later it was

---

[3] George R. Terry, *Principles of Management*, Richard D. Irwin, Inc. (1960).

$3,000 poorer and the proud possessor of a large and beautifully embossed book of procedures which had no real application for it. On the other hand, there are many medium-sized firms which have grown haphazardly and are badly in need of system, method, and uniformity; where a skillfully planned and executed procedures program can literally make the difference in creating a profit or a loss.

In the motivational climate, simple and readable procedures are considered normal. The rule of thumb, literally converted to the everyday slogan which we have already cited in these pages, is this: "If it *can* be misunderstood, it *will* be misunderstood," thereby placing a premium on simplicity. The tough-minded administrator tolerates nothing less; fat, juicy words and phrases are labeled as the work of the immature. It is surprising how effective this emphasis can be if upper management really believes in it and practices it.

Memoranda—Why?

Memos need be discussed only briefly, since the very nature of the motivational climate sets forth patterns of action which correct many of the ills caused by mass-produced memoranda prepared largely for affectation or defense. The real purpose of memos should, however, be clarified, primarily because a whole new generation of management people have received their administrative baptism under circumstances that are often muddy.

Down-to-earth, results-getting memos, then, should usually consist of—

1. A clear statement of purpose and expectation.
2. A single listing of pertinent findings.
3. A recommended, or directed, course of action—depending on who the writer is and whether he is addressing himself to a superior or a subordinate.
4. Only words or phrases directly related to some form of positive accomplishment.
5. Control dates and quantities which provide stretch.

Effective Interviewing

There are various kinds of interviews: job-seeking, counseling, disciplinary, research, medical-diagnosis, others. Common denominators in most of them are the use of words, the seeking and providing of information, and the determination of patterns of action for accomplishment.

Some people are highly effective interviewers, and some are miserable. What makes the difference? We all have the same basic word resources. True, some of us know more words than others, but there are people with immense vocabularies who are still inept in the face-to-face relationship. I have conducted many "post-interview" interviews to determine what constitutes a productive personal relationship where real rapport is established. Here are some rambling, but seasoned, observations:

1. The skillful use of words often does more harm than good unless you believe in, feel, and *are* what you say.
2. A contrived or insincere interest in the other person rarely yields the best results. Such insincerity is usually sensed even when it is not consciously realized.
3. There are words which make the other person feel a quickening of the pulse. All relatively normal people want to live long, and they want to be healthy. So—try words which are morbid, turbid, sordid, sickly, silly, or moribund and note both the conscious and the unconscious pulling-away which results. On the other hand, watch the reaction to words which smack of growth, zest, pep, sprightliness, expansion, health, and sparkle.

It should go without saying, however, that the results you get—while better—will be limited if you use even the best-chosen words for their sake alone. Rather, make people feel a sense of stretch and growth in direct response to the dynamically conceived words you use.

How to Sell with Words

Positive, ethical selling is of course a highly worthwhile part of our culture and economy. It needs no apology. We should, in fact, apologize because we have not done enough global selling of our way of life. Once we build a $40 million dam in a "backward" country, we tend to assume our job is done; we seldom point it out with justifiable pride for the rest of the world to see. Russia, on the other hand, has built many dams and roads abroad that cost a fraction of

$40 million, yet everyone who benefits from the dam or walks down the road sees clear reminders of where it came from.

Some of the real stumbling blocks to selling, both in and outside the company, at home and abroad, are these often tiresome phrases: [4]

"Let's get back to reality."
"You're 'way ahead of your time."
"You can't teach an old dog new tricks."
"The public would never go for it."
"It's against our policy."
"Let's table it for now."
"Has anyone else tried it?"
"We'll be a laughingstock."
"We've never done it before."
"That's not our problem."
"Why change? We're doing O.K."
"Don't be ridiculous!"
"We're too small (or too big) for it."
"We don't have the time."
"It isn't in the budget."
"It won't work in our department."
"The boss will never buy it."
"Let's have a dialog" (rather than "communication" as defined in this book).

The tough-minded administrator faces up squarely to this kind of objection. He stresses simple, direct words in setting forth required end results, key operating information, and control dates and quantities.

As in interviewing, the questioning technique is valuable. If you ask a series of penetrating, probing questions about reasons for the objection, the negative thinker will usually either gain new insight and alter his stand or show you that he really does have a point. In either instance, the bottleneck is eliminated.

One of the great examples of what selling with words can accomplish is the U.S. Marine Corps. New recruits learn quickly that they are members of a select, disciplined, tough outfit that gets things done. Heard, often for the first time, are words like *esprit de*

[4] Many of these remarks are taken from David L. Yunich, *How to Kill Progress*, The Economic Press (1958).

corps and *semper fidelis*. They learn about the traditions and accomplishments of the Marines. They are made to feel, through both words and actions, that discipline, hardship, and even suffering are things to be proud of, to look forward to, that virtually nothing is impossible. And just look at the results!

Contrast this with the inevitable reaction to words stressing security, a snug berth, pleasure, permissive discipline, and "happiness." Clearly, the net result will usually be the precise opposite of satisfaction or pride. The complacent, easy-going, purposeless work group becomes a bunch of backbiting malcontents.

Sell with words, then, and stay healthily impatient with your proficiency.

The Word Picture

There is a distinct difference between the spellbinding, silver-tongued orator and the person who can paint a truly fine word picture. At first blush, they appear to be the same, but let's take a closer look. The mesmerizing orator may put together ringing phrases which produce a warm glow and a desire to jump into the air and cheer. The sobering question must often be asked, however, "What shall I *do* about it?"

A good many articulate members of management groups adroitly play to the gallery in numerous types of meetings. By making frequent use of some of the action concepts we have discussed, they may even be able to achieve something. More often, however, the executive whose grasp of words is restricted to their use in emotional appeal, and who cannot follow through in a practical way, eventually encounters rough going.

If your word picture contains sound, meaty administrative substance, the contribution of action words and concepts can be considerable.

He's a Smart Man, but . . .

We have all seen people who are articulate and persuasive, who seem to have a good understanding of the management process, but who never really come into their own. What is often lacking here is intellectual and emotional discipline.

The obligation to develop and use such self-discipline increases in more than direct proportion to over-all management responsibility and persuasive skill. For, as one advances up the managerial ladder, there is increased potential for misleading and harming large numbers of people. There is, for example, the sales manager, gifted in both personal salesmanship and the motivation of subordinates, who can quickly "skim the cream" by rapidly merchandising an inadequate product.

Discipline, self-control, business statesmanship—all are needed to implement the tenets of tough-minded management. Finally, "dialog" means two or more people engaging in monologs. "Communication" means shared feeling—shared understanding.

A specific recommendation: If *all* managers—all leaders—took just a few hours to read the books of Dr. S. I. Hayakawa on semantics, the over-all benefits would be enormous.

11

The ultimate price of deception.

Phonies Finish
Last

Ours is a nation that was founded and made great by people who faced adversity squarely and waded in swinging. Yet there were, even then, phonies and leeches who were looking for something for nothing—people who detoured around the real work to be done.

What is a phony and what makes the person that way? A phony is simply someone who purports to be something he or she isn't. A phony often waits for somebody creative or tough-minded to conceive a thought or project, and then determines what can be done to benefit from it. He or she sometimes works hard, but toward no wholesome or positive end. Here is what is usually missing in such a person:

1. A clear understanding of integrity.
2. A feeling of purpose and dignity.
3. A desire to help others grow.
4. The ability and willingness to practice candor.
5. A readiness to focus on what is good about a person or thing.

6. Determination to do a job rather than simply pursue pleasure.
7. A desire to avoid the difficult and to opt for the expedient.
8. The habit of living one's beliefs, making them real convictions rather than merely giving them lip service.
9. Capacity for thinking and acting as an individual—but using this strong individuality for corporate or group accomplishment.
10. The rare qualities of courage and vulnerability.
11. Sufficient self-confidence.

It is particularly significant in this context to read many of the current "smart" and "avant-garde" magazines. Here we see truly skilled journalists applying their biting and incisive phrases to much that is currently American. And what direction do these journalistic pyrotechnics take? Largely, they seize on what is wrong with the country: its people, its customs, and its efforts. This may be titillating, but what on earth is it accomplishing? If the same talents were used to set forth national goals, the full extent of our resources, the accomplishments and potential of our business people and many other hard-working groups, we would not find it so often necessary to label ourselves phonies.

It is important to cast lack of values, callousness and even brutality, sheeplike behavior, and spineless amorality in their real roles:

1. Show the blustering, brutal top executive who openly sneers that the only way to handle subordinates is to make them fear you as the insecure, befuddled, weak person he really is.
2. Show the smooth, fiction-type young comer who relies for advancement on looks and personality alone as the retarded, out-of-date misfit she is.
3. Show the employee whose only concern is to protect a job at the expense of others as the parasite he is.
4. Show the sarcastic cynic as the coward he usually is. "You must *be* something before you can *say* something."
5. Show the gaily unscrupulous company person with everything, seemingly, coming his way not as the all-conquering hero but as the uncertain, groping, sometimes pathetic figure he is.

If you, the executive, are in a top job now by virtue of being a phony and a politician, take stock of yourself. The future can still be salvaged if you begin quickly to get some blocks of granite under you.

Who's Fooling Whom?

A man often starts looking for the easy and devious way as a child. Then, as he grows older, it's comforting to say:

"I'm doing this for my wife and kids."
"If *I* don't stick the knife in, somebody else will."
"Business is a jungle. You've got to be tough to survive."
"Once I get on top, I'll change."
"I'm only getting even."

But who's fooling whom? You know, your spouse knows, and others know what really put you in the executive suite. The chances are that your spouse is nervous and neurotic by now as a result of your machinations. Will a new home or a trip to Bermuda make up for these wrongs? The tough-minded executive knows the answer.

I recently read about a group of prep-school youths who have labeled themselves *neg-o's*. Those boys come from some of the "best" families in the United States. They say a *neg-o* is a person who has nothing to believe in—who feels the price of business success is too high—who has no desire at all to grow up and be like his parents.

Two things could be wrong here: (1) The parents really aren't very desirable people, or (2) they haven't built lasting values and mental discipline into their children—or both. It is alleged that the *neg-o* movement is growing. If this is true, it is a pretty good answer to the phony when he asks himself, "Who's fooling whom?"

The Price Is High

Is this no more than meaningless indictment—the kind of finger pointing we have already frowned on? No! Our concern, though, is with what the tough-minded manager can do about it.

You must understand first that the price for soft-minded slackness is very high. We are talking about much more than the success of any one company or individual. For, if our nation crumbles from within because of satiation, fatty heart, and hardened arteries, we shall have failed to meet our obligations to the rest of the world.

It is fashionable to say that the world is changing fast, but I wonder whether the average American really has any idea *how* fast. Self-concern, phoniness, laziness, preoccupation with pleasure can literally nail us in a hurry. The other peoples of the world, with particular emphasis on the men in the Kremlin, have no reason to feel compassion for us if they can best us in the world's marketplaces. *And they would like to do it.*

Why Dignity?

What is dignity and why is it important to the tough-minded executive? The essential nature of this quality is widely misunderstood today and has been for years. Many otherwise intelligent and wise people still tend to equate dignity with solemnity, white hair, the burden of years, transcendent or haughty air, majestic carriage, conservative dress, slowness to show enthusiasm about anything new. This concept does not hold water today and never did; the basic character of a person is not that superficial. Who has not seen people that, on close scrutiny, are pretty unscrupulous, small, and negative yet display many of the popular manifestations of "dignity"?

According to the dictionary, "dignity" implies elevation of character, intrinsic worth, excellence. It is what you *are*. It includes many of the qualities we have seen are vital to success that is based on more than a foundation of sand:

1. A full measure of individuality—the guts to be yourself.
2. An unwillingness to compromise with half-truths and foggy interpretations of morality.
3. A genuine concern for the growth, development, and happiness of others.
4. Humbleness toward God and confidence in one's abilities. They are indivisible!
5. A real desire to *accomplish* something; the recognition that actions without results are not only unbusinesslike but downright disillusioning.

Build on Granite

Most of the weaknesses in our national clay stem from a general climate which is lacking in sufficient purpose, direction, and know-how. Tough-minded administrators in both business and public institutions can do much to change this.

They must, above all, be impatient with phonies. They must remember, however, that many company politicians and wielders of the knife will not shape up in response to mild appeals for integrity. It must be made clear that their maneuverings will not be tolerated, and this in turn requires that top executives exemplify dignity and integrity in their personal conduct. They will need keen perception and astuteness, backed by a coordinated, cohesive approach—not one that is structured or segmented. Clear definition of company and departmental objectives, of individual goals and purpose; an honest effort at sound communications; an atmosphere in which candor and empathy flourish—all the components of the motivational climate are, in fact, the blocks of granite needed by the tough-minded executive.

The same concepts and practices which have stood the test in progressive companies can bring a sorely needed shot of adrenalin to our society as a whole. The most natural starting point for the conscientious top executive is right at home; he must first make sure he is running an organization which is getting things done as a team. The person who does an outstanding job for his or her company will almost certainly find many opportunities to fill a broader role.

The End of the Story

Most seasoned business people can point to those who have climbed the corporate ladder by walking over more capable competitors, who have mastered a variety of subtle and skillful techniques for securing promotions. Understandably, then, earnest admonitions about what happens to phonies are bound to encounter reactions to this effect:

> "Look at So-and-So! He's one of our vice presidents, and nothing's about to happen to *him?*"
> "There was this smoothie in our company who sold herself so well that she's just left to become president of another company."

We could cite such instances by the dozen. Usually, however, a careful check shows that these people get their comeuppance in one way or another. There undoubtedly are a number of cases where little sign of the inevitable can be discerned at the present time, but the end of the story has not yet been written.

The tough-minded executive views all this in perspective. He knows that the ultimate price must somehow be paid. Tough-minded managers are beginning to recognize the detrimental dimensions of the "jockstrap syndrome" in our society. Unless a person builds a life on a value system rooted in daring, caring, and sharing rather than becoming a pathetic "middle-aged locker room boy" he drifts into early obsolescence. It is so crucial that we as a nation clearly identify and define a *real* man and a *real* woman so that *real* (not phony) relationships can happen.

I submit here some traits for the guidance of the men and women who want to lead *real* lives. They must:

> Care much.
> Dare much.
> Share much.
> Stretch much.
> Expect much.
> Give much.
> Live much.
> Love much.
> Grow much.
> Experiment much.
> Seek challenges and obstacles.
> Have a sense of wonder.
> Have a specific program of physical, mental, and spiritual fitness.
> Constantly pursue a greater awareness of his or her own strengths.
> Constantly pursue new knowledge of the strengths of others.
> Make the quantum leap from "judging" others on the basis of their weaknesses to "evaluating" them according to their present and potential strengths.

Implicit in these expectations may be the *hope* needed to respond to the poignant lament of Alexander Solzhenitsyn, who describes the Western world as spiritually exhausted.

12

Candor: applied honesty.

The Essential Lubricant

Is it realistic to look for one all-pervasive approach to management? Is there common grist for every mill? One formula or approach that will solve everything? Probably not, but there *is* one common denominator without which management cannot be truly effective.

Time and again management has prematurely identified problems as marketing, apathetic executives, lack of motivation on the part of subordinates, excessive costs, need for budgets, poor personnel management. And sometimes one of these turns out to be the real problem area. There may, however, be one single missing factor underlying all such difficulties.

Symptomatic statements like these are often heard:

"I thought they understood what I meant."
"Why, that is clearly stated in the Procedures Manual!"
"I work hard, but no one recognizes it."
"Why do I have to provide all the new ideas?"
"Even with job descriptions and manuals of all kinds, they don't seem to know what I expect."
"We're going to have to fire a few people; then things will shape up."
"I have to do everything myself or it doesn't get done."

"I try to be a nice guy, but firing or something may be the only solution."

"I'm going to junk what I learned in that human relations course and go back to cracking the whip."

These are not isolated or infrequent remarks; they are heard in uneasy profusion from coast to coast. Moreover, solution of the problems they represent is seldom easy—it requires courage, vision, and empathy. What is missing, in short, is candor, which should not be confused with mere bluntness, frankness, or coarseness but should be viewed as *applied honesty*.

Face to Face

A clear recognition of the need for candor must start with the top executive. He often objects, "I think too much of my people to be that frank with them." He must understand, however, that he is not *deferring* to the basic dignity of his subordinates when he relies solely on diplomacy, hints, innuendo, and slyness or on job descriptions and memos; he is *ignoring* it.

Much of what is done in the name of diplomacy and pleasantness is simply prevarication and/or an unwillingness to face up to a difficult situation. The executive who will not practice candor or applied integrity in the face-to-face relationship is seldom motivated by "kindness"; rather, he is unwilling to subject himself to the resulting emotional strains. Tough-mindedness is imperative here. The person with this quality is big enough to endure the emotional rigors that may accompany the session; she realizes these will be outweighed by the benefits the other person will derive from new insight and knowledge about his strengths and weaknesses.

The president of a chemical company hired a new marketing vice president. He was sure that this move would do much for the future of the company. Careful preparations were made for the new arrival: a thorough position description was compiled; a clear statement of company objectives was worked out, with particular emphasis on marketing; complete information with regard to past precedents and experiences was assembled; budgetary and other pertinent material was placed at the disposal of the new vice president. On arrival, he busied himself talking with people, preparing written documents, laying enthusiastic plans, and generating a lot of activity. The president confidently looked for great things to start happening; and, even when few signs of improvement could be discerned, he resolved to stay out of the picture and give the vice president ample opportunity to display his talents. The marketing VP began to feel that the president took very little interest in the marketing side of the business; after all, he spoke in only the most general and euphemistic terms whenever they got together.

As the months went by, each began to feel the other was not genuinely interested or motivated. This unfortunate but not unusual situation had reached the point where the president was on the verge of dismissing the new VP when steps were taken to bring about a complete and candid exchange of information between the two. The "bowing and scraping," the nice, kindly manifestations of courtesy and good will, and the other artificial mannerisms that stood in the way of effective communication were replaced by a candid, freewheeling, businesslike concentration on results. The vice president earned his salary, and the president was satisfied.

The often-repeated statement, "We pay him a good salary, so he ought to *know* what to do," has the ring of sheer futility.

Committees and Candor

There is an old saw that a camel is a horse put together by a committee. And, in fact, any discussion of committees kindles diverse reactions ranging from stout defense to complete contempt. Committees have their purpose—and they often function well if properly conceived, organized, and controlled. On the other hand, they are often convenient vehicles for tabling difficult problems or deferring unpopular action.

Let's put substance and meaning into our use of committees by—

1. Painstakingly clarifying the purpose of the committee.
2. Making sure all members understand the *what, where, when, who, how,* and *why* of the committee.
3. Scheduling meetings so that the members will not have their minds on bread-and-butter activities or be fatigued or otherwise muddled.
4. Conditioning all conversation and plans with a strong flavor of results desired, not just actions involved.
5. Securing full participation and identification by all members.
6. Guarding against trivial outside distractions.
7. Using the problem-solving technique as a general guide to a flexible *modus operandi.*

8. Setting control dates and quantities to provide stretch in achieving committee objectives.
9. Avoiding banal attempts on the part of members to play to the gallery or simply to please each other.
10. Placing a premium on simplicity and end results.

These requirements of a good committee should help illustrate the necessity of candor. I recall a committee meeting set up for trouble-shooting purposes where the sales manager threw this problem out for discussion: "One of my better salespeople has been over-charging the company on the expense account for years—I've given him some broad hints at sales meetings, and he just doesn't get the drift. What can I do?" The group came up with such solutions as these: "Fire him—he's dishonest!" "Hint more strongly." "Show each man's total expenses at the next sales meeting; he'll feel small and will probably change." "Place an arbitrary limit on their expenses and inform them of it in writing."

The discussion went on till one committee member used the questioning technique and asked whether the man had ever been counseled thoroughly on the results requirements of his job, on the procedures and ethics involved, on the philosophy and objectives of the department, and so on. The answer was, "No, he's a good sales-person, and all that red tape might make him quit." However, the sales manager was persuaded to try counseling—with surprising success. Angered by the boss's hints and suspicions, the salesperson had indeed been on the point of quitting and, after a long and candid discussion of the situation, was vastly relieved. He hadn't even known the company's policy on expense accounts and hadn't the vaguest notion why the sales manager seemed critical. Through the new insight which he and his superior both achieved, he became more than just a good salesperson—he became outstanding.

This is a double-barreled example of how a committee can be effective only if it is interacting dynamically and candidly and how an employee can perform properly only if management will make its expectations known beyond any possible doubt.

Counsel—Don't Advise

Many people react warmly and positively to counsel and just the opposite to advice. What's the difference? I have worked with lawyers who didn't know; as a result, they gave advice when counsel was needed and then wondered why the client relationship did not blossom as anticipated. Distinguishing between the two terms is easy, but carrying out the concept in practice requires some doing.

Advising is telling other people what they should do. *Counseling* is enabling them to see what should be done, how, and why; it also requires that they feel motivated to use the counsel. (This is one key criterion for distinguishing the successful lawyer from the unsuccessful.) The counselor must have insight, empathy, perception, warmth, and wisdom. The adviser needs only intelligence. When seasoned counsel is provided within a context of consideration for the growth and benefit of the counselee, candor can seldom be overdone.

You may *advise* your production manager that a work simplification program should be in operation three months from now. The results of this advice may be uncertain. You may *counsel* your production manager by requesting his best thinking on the need for such a program, getting him to tell you how and why it should be done as well as when. You are not surrendering your prerogative as his superior because you can still modify his proposed date in light of your greater knowledge of over-all requirements. You gain much, however, both by benefiting from his specialized knowledge and experience and by letting him identify himself with end results and commitments.

Rough Going for Politics

It is a basic tenet of tough-minded management that we face up to every situation, no matter how tenuous, and talk it out. We must exemplify this by focusing on a subject that is seldom labeled and discussed openly and candidly. That subject is "company politics" with its many shadings and overtones, its cliques and pressures, its insidious and poisonous effects on productivity.

What causes this ulcer-producing and debilitating situation? Employees, up to and including the president, seldom practice politics in a cold, calculated desire to be diabolical. This is a response triggered by fear and its natural corollary, emotional insecurity.

Several years ago, the personnel administrator of an aircraft company participated in many grievance hearings in an atmosphere that was charged with union-management tensions. On several occasions, union stewards attempted to drive a wedge between the personnel administrator and his assistant by alleging that the assistant was saying and doing certain things to eliminate the boss and get the boss's job. In each instance, however, the personnel administrator quickly went to the telephone and asked the assistant to come to the conference room. When he arrived, the allegations were quickly withdrawn by the union stewards. Candor in this situation avoided unhealthy, political overtones. The personnel administrator might easily have concluded that he was being secretly attacked and taken action detrimental to everyone concerned.

In our constant search for what seem to be increasingly complex and esoteric management tools, it is often easy to overlook the simple and obvious fact that there is no substitute for the straightforward and understanding use of *truth*. Political maneuvering has rough going in a climate where management by objectives, or results, is operative; where candor and clear communication are practiced; and where a clear understanding of individual role and purpose exists. It is vital, however, that candor become "the thing" and that the reasons why be communicated from above.

The Prevalence of Yes Men

Among the creeping, pervasive effects of lack of candor is the prevalence of yes men. (To be entirely fair about it, we must acknowledge the fact that women, too, can qualify.) The executive who recognizes that he is failing to capitalize on his most valuable potential sources of innovation because of submissive, pliant subordinates should take a hard look at himself and determine whether he may be to blame. Much of the time we find yes men reporting to a dynamic top executive who really wants a creative, articulate, courageous group of people. In many such instances he has done a poor job of selection, has dominated his subordinates unduly, or simply has not made it clear by word and *deed* that no penalty of any kind will be forthcoming as long as a subordinate, before expressing a candid opinion, has brought his or her best thinking and talents to bear on the problem being considered.

This kind of top executive may be very sincere about wanting all the benefits to be derived from a dynamic group of non-conformists. But he either doesn't want or doesn't know how to build the climate which produces them.

Jumping across a broad chasm without building a bridge is seldom possible. Attempting to change conformist-type, permissive people into hard-hitting producers overnight is equally unrealistic, yet it is amazing how often people who are otherwise highly intelligent, or even brilliant, think this can be done. The planks in the bridge across the chasm are the components of the total motivational climate.

The yes man must shape up or get out of the company, or department, headed by the tough-minded manager. He is sometimes carried out! I remember a yes man who had maneuvered himself into a position greater than his ability warranted. His new standard of living made it important to stay there, and his subsequent anxieties caused him to become, among other things, a compulsive eater. The impact of all this new weight and tension brought about a heart attack at the age of forty-seven. After recovering, to took a lesser job in a different company, where his wise boss helped him to understand himself better, to see the fundamental necessity of integrity, to take the job seriously but not himself. A career and a life were resurrected through the courage of a tough-minded boss.

It is a mark of wisdom to recognize that failure to face an issue squarely never solves anything—it only buys time.

Businesses Are Composed of People

Earlier in this book we pointed out that people—specifically employees—adjust more easily to innovation than some authorities claim. This is certainly true if the change comes from the outside, as when new machines are bought for the office or automation comes to the factory. At the same time it should be recognized that few adults take readily to the need for change within themselves. It follows, therefore, that if personnel in an organization do not see the benefit to themselves of candor and frankness, they almost certainly will not practice them. This brings us squarely to a logical sequence of focal points:

1. People in general are reluctant to change and acquire new and unfamiliar habits and attitudes. Furthermore, they will not change unless they know *why* they must.
2. Business organizations, as they acquire new methods, procedures, products, and equipment, must change their attitudes and values.
3. Business organizations are composed of people.
4. People will continue to resist changing if fed a diet of blandness, niceties, and banalities. Therefore:

5. Candor is the essential lubricant for clear, lucid communication between subordinates, associates, and superiors. If you neither require nor help a person to face up to the realities of his job, his goals, his resources and potential, he simply is not in the best position to function as a well-integrated person and to make a maximum contribution to the company.

It should be clear to the thinking executive that there is no substitute for applied integrity or honesty—in *all* dimensions of the organization.

Stimulating Constructive Innovation

Without innovation, a business regresses. This means—to repeat—innovation in people, attitudes, values, and goals as well as processes, products, equipment, and facilities. How does the motivational climate, with its emphasis on candor, stimulate constructive innovation?

1. Candor is instrumental in removing inhibitions and clarifying foggy concepts—two things which often impede the development and implementation of new ideas.
2. Candor encourages, even requires, an emphasis on truth, and the search for truth has been responsible for all really great innovations since the beginning of man.
3. Candor rules out an emphasis on activities or "busyness" and focuses on results. Aimless, unmotivated activity seldom produces innovation.
4. Candor brings all the resources of the business to bear on the achievement of company objectives. Unnecessary staff, unused space, superfluous procedures cannot survive.
5. Candor requires that the research and development staff be justified in terms of profitability. The benefits to innovation here are obvious. Fussy, pedantic people who are dabbling do not last long.
6. Candor as a business way of life helps insure that mistakes or misdirected energies will be righted much earlier—with a consequent saving of time and energy for more positive use.
7. Candor, with the accompanying freedom to make mistakes, plays a powerful role in unleashing the creative talents of the more timorous and even the more courageous employee.

The well-managed company must move in the vanguard of the search for innovation. This means that the stretching, questing attitudes which the motivational climate is designed to produce will be even more important to business tomorrow as our role in the world marketplace is altered by shortened global communications and increasingly tough competition.

The Only Way

The sales manager of a metal-fabricating business was a gregarious life-of-the-party type. He started sales meetings by firing a pistol into the air, singing a ditty, or attempting some other superficial attention-getter. More seriously, he could quote extensively from many of the popular books on salesmanship. But sales volume left much to be desired.

A study of the organization showed that no standards existed for determining the worth or contribution of any major function in the company. Moreover, while the sales manager was a popular and likable fellow, he was not consistent, and his salesmen had gradually gotten into the habit of ignoring much of what he said or at best procrastinating when given instructions. He seemed chronically allergic to any kind of conversation with a subordinate which involved facing facts and talking them through. Accountability, he thought, was great—but it developed that he believed a statement in writing, telling a man to produce or else, constituted accountability. Faced with the need to establish sound performance criteria and personally discuss with subordinates the results of consistent failure to meet commitments, he recoiled.

When, however, he realized that this was the only positive and healthy thing to do, that it took more courage to listen well and to counsel objectively than it did to fire a man or chew him out, he'd taken his first step toward growth. As time went on, the total sales effort improved greatly, and the sales manager became an effective administrator. His biggest stumbling block had been that he imagined a candid face-to-face discussion had to carry negative overtones.

Actually, it was a matter of facing up to the need for frankness and honesty in achieving positive results. The tough-minded manager does not bear witness to honesty simply in church or at company picnics. He plays the whole game honestly; candor, he knows, in personal day-to-day relationships is the only real way.

Most major executives could learn much from a lady who is small in physical stature but a giant in wisdom and perception. Here is what Anne Morrow Lindbergh shares with us: "The most exhausting thing in life is insincerity."

I hope all readers will ponder these words deeply. There is something about large and generous doses of *truth* that free up the mind and spirit for greater growth, productivity, interpersonal effectiveness, and just plain *happiness*. Are you courageous enough—do you *care* enough to become a student—a scholar—of the truth? The payoff is enormous! It is so eminently *practical*.

13 *Concentration on self-development*
will help insure wiser use of authority.

Courage and Logic

There has been much talk in recent years about whether management is an art, a profession, or a science. Or is it just an ungainly outgrowth of a past era of small shops and general stores when the main key to prosperity seemed to be, "Buy low and sell high"?

The exponents of "professional" management point to the fact that the operators of most modern businesses are no longer owners and are not entrepreneurs in the old, accepted use of the term—that the modern top executive is in the top spot because he was able to make effective use of a whole kit of sophisticated management tools. The need for a code of ethics for management has also been cited as evidence that it is a budding profession.

So—is the typical executive in the modern organization a professional, a scientist, an entrepreneur, a hybrid, or what? More often than not, he doesn't regard himself as any of these; rather, he sees himself as a person who has worked hard to help his company prosper and has emerged as top man by virtue of this effort. Sometimes he has scientifically organized the humanity right out of the job to the extent possible, fancying himself as pretty much of an omnipotent human computer who has learned to marshal people and things to do his bidding. In other instances he has carefully developed an organization which leaves him relatively free to manage by exception. This is usually good; but it can be overdone, if a middle layer of committees and management fat is allowed to develop, to the point where everything is solved by group dynamics.

When the smoke blows away, we find two characteristics that are almost always present in the successful manager. These are courage and logic. Courage can often be equated in a broad sense with honesty and integrity, and logic with the decision-making process. They are both necessary parts of the tough-minded executive's *modus operandi*.

New Styles in Bossism

The boss system in business has never really met the test of enlightened management. The old-time boss ruled by force and threats—and usually was obeyed. But obedience is not enough. Many wives who obey their husbands do not necessarily love and honor them.

The manager of a large department store was a big black-browed man who ruled all eight floors of the store with an iron hand. All the employees were very much afraid of him because he had been known to fire people on the smallest provocation. But the stockboys, floorwalkers, and salesclerks found many clever ways to kill time, and they were almost happy when defective merchandise was returned because this, in some way, was a blow at the manager.

When he retired, the new manager who was sent in was small and unimpressive in appearance; he seldom raised his voice and was slow to anger. Other business people predicted that he would fail miserably in trying to match his predecessor's record.

He began by requesting all the employees to fill in a confidential questionnaire in which they were asked for their complete and candid opinions about the past, present, and future operation of the store. They were also asked to list their personal goals and reasons for working. He made sure through bulletin boards, letters to the home, and other media that everyone knew precisely why the store was in business and what it might accomplish in the next five years. Results requirements were developed for each job. Each department within the store was put on a profitability basis. Personal development sessions were held with key people. When they made negative and acid comments about the previous manager, the new man heard them out and then suggested what to *do* to make the future better.

At first there was very little change; but, as the various parts of the new approach began to spark and fuse together, morale rose rapidly. Some negative attitudes lingered for a long while, and some people who were not comfortable in an environment where results were the prime criteria left. At the end of the first year of operation under the new man, the net profit was higher than it had ever been under the old regime.

Here was a "boss" whose use of both warmth and discipline stamped him as truly tough-minded although in every other way he was the antithesis of a "tough acting" person.

What are the implications of this background for modern management? The lessons of history are clear. Benevolent paternalism, autocratic methods, permissiveness—none of these has really stood up. On the other hand, history is loaded with examples of what can be accomplished by groups of people who are motivated by enlightened self-interest and a desire to work.

As we have said repeatedly, one of the great fallacies of modern times is that people do not want to work. If this were true, autocratic, bull-of-the-woods tactics would probably still be in wide use and would perhaps be the best type of management. But it is not true, and management in many cases has committed grave errors in judgment by negotiating union contracts on this basis and otherwise relying on it.

More Pull than Push

An interesting but sometimes uneasy question for an executive to ask is, "Could I still get respect and performance from the people around me if I weren't the boss?" This kind of self-appraisal can be very useful if properly pursued because it helps to etch sharply the basic qualities of the person. Even though he obviously does not plan to shed any of his authority, concentration on the development of greater courage and logic will help insure wiser use of it.

American management and supervisory personnel have been caught in a mainstream of self-examination and change ever since World War II. It has been popular to say that the modern manager must be a leader and not a driver, that pull accomplishes more than push. But we need to examine why this may be true and how it works.

When human beings first evolved, they were distinguished from lower forms of life primarily by their upright carriage and their superior ability to think and communicate. Perhaps most important was their ability to exercise judgment and to achieve an autonomous and relatively complete family unit. The desire to be self-reliant and self-sufficient has stood out strongly across the centuries. There have been leaders; but these have usually been, first of all, strong individuals and, secondly, uniters of other individuals for group achievement.

The Course of Least Resistance

These considerations should provide the modern manager with some *why*'s to sustain him in various crises. Courage and logic are at a premium because it can be so easy to follow the course of least resistance. For example:

1. Using bluster and threats instead of firm, consistent requests.
2. Pulling rank instead of facing up to a problem and talking it out. Using rank as your first expedient.
3. Firing people as a first resort prior to attempting to build them.
4. Procrastinating about firing people when a logical analysis indicates it must be done.
5. Dealing with a subordinate on the basis of what he did *wrong* rather than what he should do that is more nearly *right*.
6. Telling others your problems rather than your solutions. Buck passing requires no courage whatsoever and certainly doesn't meet the requirements of logic.
7. Evading a particular discussion or action because it is painful to *you*. Candor is often avoided for this reason rather than a genuine desire to spare the other person. The cold facts are that the other person will almost always benefit from candor if it is genuinely intended in his best interests and tailored to fulfill his individual needs for recognition, security, opportunity, and belonging.
8. Using sarcasm and oblique witticisms to squelch others rather than an orderly, sympathetic approach to achieving a solution.
9. Agreeing with others simply because it is more expedient.
10. Sticking to the status quo because change takes time and energy.

11. Rewarding subordinates for such things as club membership, family connections, old school ties, and politicking rather than for contribution to company objectives.
12. Other understandable temptations to take the easy way out.

It should be helpful in resisting these habits and patterns to examine the history of the world, noting how the rise of nations and whole civilizations has been made possible by enlightened, hard-working, and positively motivated people—and how, contrariwise, their fall has been hastened by self-indulgence, negative attitudes, and lack of willingness to face up to many kinds of reality.

Take the case where the decision to dismiss a person is a distinctly positive and therapeutic step. There are countless instances where failure to face up to this task and follow through on it has caused irreparable harm. The following example is one of far too many.

A company president decided one of his vice presidents must go. Because the man had numerous friends in the industry and was well liked by his associates, delicate handling seemed indicated; so the decision was made to freeze him out. His subordinates were quietly instructed to bypass him on all major matters but to defer to him on minor decisions. He was gradually omitted from the distribution list for major memoranda and announcements and was no longer asked to key meetings. He tried to find out what was wrong but ran into such politeness and diplomacy at every turn that he wound up completely frustrated. His feelings ran the gamut from initial exasperation to such utter discouragement and despair that he suffered a nervous breakdown. Had the president found the courage to deal with him directly, the aplomb of both men might have been shaken, but the vice president would most likely have avoided the nervous breakdown and the net result to the company would have been less unfavorable.

Another top executive, noted for his diplomacy and suave polish, called a subordinate in just before she was due to start her vacation and exposed her to many phrases such as: "One must recognize that on occasion a company must do things that do not lend themselves readily to clarification. . . ." He assumed he had gently eased the subordinate out, but the woman had not gotten the message at all. Upon returning from vacation, she found her office occupied by a stranger and everybody proceeding on the assumption that she had been dismissed. The ensuing confusion was both unnecessary and humiliating to all parties. Candor, courage, and logic—seasoned with warmth and empathy—would have been not only the tough-minded way but, clearly, the only civilized way.

Don't Fetter Your Imagination

Throughout our country and perhaps throughout the world, millions of man-hours are wasted in aimless yearnings and aspirations which dissipate energy and never culminate in real accomplishment. Consider the executive who told me he seldom went to sleep at night without first lying awake for two or three hours trying to work out new angles for getting rich. Asked what he did to make this dreaming come true, he said wanly, "Nothing. I never have the energy to follow through." Ironic? Yes, but not uncommon. System, method, and order are not as inherent in the typical executive as many people suppose.

It has become increasingly popular to assume that imaginative and dynamic things will happen when a major position is filled by a person who possesses, roughly, the following qualifications: at least one college degree (preferably two, sometimes three or more); considerable related experience; pleasant and personable mannerisms; and the ability to assuage feelings and pour oil on troubled waters. Many times a person with these flawless credentials is recruited and placed in charge of a department with high accompanying expectations. However, if he moves into a nonmotivational climate and simply continues to be a nice guy with flawless credentials, he usually doesn't get the job done.

The latent imagination which exists in just about everybody can be unleashed only if the results required of each position clearly demand the constructive use of imagination. Individual talents must have specific targets within a climate of totally targeted activity. Individuals must see some real relationship between their own yearnings and the accomplishments of their department and company.

Without this targeted thinking, results are often dissipated, unchanneled, and unproductive.

Problem Solving in the Motivational Climate

Problem solving in the motivational climate is somewhat different in nature although similar in general technique to the traditional method of defining the problem, establishing the objectives, getting the facts, studying the facts, taking action, and evaluating the results of the action.

One difference is that the past is not the all-important determinant of what should be done in the future. Trends and curves are not the only basis for planning. Rather, certain problems are more easily solved because management planning *makes them arise sooner and at a more convenient time.* How is this done? One requirement is that the tough-minded company not wait for its particular industry to set a pattern—that it help forge the shape of the pattern.

This takes courage, and it takes logic. It needn't, however, be financially perilous. Many companies are greatly minimizing risk by setting the pace in their industry and reaping the benefits before the less courageous competitor can react. Sears, Roebuck is an excellent example of a pace-setting company that has vigorously carried out courageous plans when others hung back. Certainly, it had problems, but these were minimized because they were often the result of premeditated hurdles. The competitor that is primarily a follower can and frequently does profit by the trials and errors of the trail blazer, but seldom to the extent that his gains equal the losses caused by his slowness in taking decisive steps forward.

The small company executive may say, "We're too little for that. Let's wait and see what the big boys are going to do." This seldom yields dividends; instead, this country is full of little companies that became big by forcing circumstances to work in their favor. Small and medium-sized companies can use their very lack of size as one of their greatest assets if they become taut ships and practice the principles of sound management. Auren Uris, of the Research Institute of America, has coined a term that is particularly appropriate in this context of problem solving. He calls it "tomorrow-mindedness."[1]

In deliberately forcing the appearance of certain problems, the right climate is necessary. Tomorrow-mindedness must permeate the whole structure. It must be popular to talk about tomorrow—not just in terms of the astronauts and Project Gemini but in terms of the methods of learning that will prevail in 1982, the obsolescence of the wheel, new dimensions of city planning, shifting theories of population control, evolving folkways, mores, and laws, and a myriad of other bits in the emerging mosaic. Further, an esprit de corps must exist throughout the company. The best market research data possible are of no particular value if the organization is not geared to provide taut, tough-minded follow-through.

[1] Auren Uris, *The Executive Deskbook,* Van Nostrand-Reinhold (1976).

Becoming

Over the years I have counseled hundreds of executives of all kinds. I have found there is a discernible difference in the value system of those who were relatively successful and those who were unusually successful.

The relatively successful person has focused on what to *do*. The unusually successful person has first and always focused on what to *be*, and only secondarily on what to *do*. The person who forms what he is *be*coming, usually finds it relatively easy to then determine what to *do*.

Most of the great thinkers and philosophers have suggested what we should *do*. Only Christ laid down a comprehensive blueprint for *be*ing. It is illuminating to contrast the relative effect or impact of each.

Who do you want to *be*?

14

Create an awareness, or develop a philosophy, that work can and should be a pleasant part of total productivity.

Work, Warmth, and Wisdom

BUILDING a team that works hard and loves it is one of the most challenging and worthwhile jobs the executive can ever undertake. And it *can* be *done*. A pivotal concept in achieving this much-to-be-desired goal is a better understanding of two of life's fundamentals:

1. Good health is to be sought and cherished as an important part of the good life.
2. Satisfying, productive work is an important, even essential part of good health.

To quote Dr. William P. Shepard:

To be selfish is one luxury the executive must deny himself. But it is not selfish to claim that his first duty is to himself.

To put a finer point on it, his first duty is to his good health. He must keep himself in perfect shape—or as close to perfect as possible. Perhaps perfection is always just one step beyond. No executive can allow himself to think he has achieved perfection. But with his health he must be close to it.

He must be not merely "okay," not "better, thanks," not "getting along." He must be robust, alert, vigorous, cheerful, and optimistic.

Look twice at the decision of the executive with an ulcer. It may not be the executive, but the ulcer, that makes the decision.

Rely not on the executive who suffers from chronic fatigue. He will postpone until tomorrow because today all he can think of is the rest he needs.[1]

Elementary Common Sense

It is just good, basic, down-to-earth, tough-minded procedure for you (and each of your employees) to maintain a proper regard for your physical and, hence, mental fitness. Healthy, orderly, and vigorous objectives are conceived by healthy, orderly, and vigorous people. And it is often a waste of time and money to concentrate on middle and lower management levels if the top person is out of phase emotionally, mentally, spiritually, or physically.

A healthy and zestful workforce is necessary to a growing, profitable, and worthwhile business. Turnover and absenteeism statistics cannot begin to capture the lackluster and negative results of a group of people who show up but move around under a pall of the "gray sickness," with no real enthusiasm for anything. Yet there are thousands and thousands of such workers in well-lighted, well-ventilated plants and offices all over the country, partly because management simply has not provided an environment that meets the employee's basic needs.

Alfred J. Marrow puts it well:

> A person who can speak his mind to his neighbors on any subject, but not to management on his work, which is what concerns him most; who can ingeniously design and "do-it-himself" at home, but is never called upon to do like things with the tools at the factory; whose job is so splintered that it is reduced to simple and dull repetitions of the same routine; whose foreman slights his views and underestimates his intelligence—no matter how well such a person is paid, or how much money he can spend for fun after hours, his frustrations are expressed by restlessness and belligerency.
>
> He may try to forget his boring job in the hypnosis of watching TV, or in long narcotic drives over the weekend, or in "do-it-yourself"

[1] William P. Shepard, M.D., *Executives' Health Secrets,* Bobbs-Merrill Company, Inc. (1961), p. 13.

tinkering that reassures him that he *can* do it himself without having a supervisor breathing down his neck. But the mass-media distractions too often merely distract without refreshing. Nor is tinkering any substitute for doing a task which makes him feel that he counts for something in the social order. The weekend passes quickly and Blue Monday comes again. He returns to work heavy-footed. And, for this, there is nobody to be mad at except management, whether the brass upstairs or the overzealous foreman or the officious supervisor.

The average American worker today still has modest enough goals in life. But he will not be satisfied if his job consists only of his performing a set series of acts like an automaton. He wants variety, he wants challenges to his skill and ingenuity, he wants to be solving some part of the problem himself, he wants more say in how things are done. How to provide this is a challenge to management.[2]

It is axiomatic that the urge to live and work creatively—so often stultified and stifled—is given free rein in the motivational climate where individual goals and purposes are clarified and blended with departmental and company goals; where individuality is nurtured by tough-minded leadership; where results are the measure of the person rather than "busyness."

Prescription for Longevity

There have been many leaders and vigorous personalities who have maintained busy schedules and active lives while in their seventies and eighties, thus attesting to the life-enriching and life-preserving qualities of work. Dr. Paul Dudley White, for example, has become the subject of numerous accounts testifying to the value of consistent physical activity.

If, as some suppose, the tensions and pressures to which executives are subjected are responsible for most of their coronary and nervous problems, why aren't physicians in the same category? They put in long hours, are subjected to consistent tension, deal constantly with life and death, and must make many hard decisions. Yet their average life span is much greater than that of the typical executive. The explanation may lie in such factors as less academic preparation and mental discipline, a less rigid selective process, and more de-

[2] Alfred J. Marrow, *Making Management Human,* McGraw-Hill Book Company (1957), p. 46.

manding environment, but these are not consistent factors and won't bear close scrutiny.

It is a contention of this book—as must be obvious by now—that one of the principal things lacking in the life of many executives is purely and simply a set of clearly defined and understood purposes, goals, or objectives. In short, their role is seldom defined in sufficient depth. A comment often heard by company physicians, even from the top man, is, "I don't know what I'm doing in this rat race." The true motivational climate requires that key management personnel *know* what they are about and where they are going before they can realistically motivate their subordinates.

Physicians have their Hippocratic oath, lawyers have their bar examinations, and the roles of both are clear. The professor has rigid requirements to meet in preparing to teach and well-prescribed strata of academic achievement. In short, most of the long-established professions have somewhat of a "calling," and their practitioners are accordingly free from many pressures and conflicting attitudes which confront the businessperson daily.

Some writers have suggested a fairly rigid codification of the management job. In the environment of the tough-minded manager, however, management must remain fluid and dynamic and must expand or change in sensitive reaction to consumer needs; moreover, that environment requires and develops a high measure of individuality—and uniformity is not consistent with our free enterprise system. Also, rigidity is anathema to tough-mindedness.

To sum up: For work to be conducive to long life, certain components of the motivational climate are manifestly imperative. These are:

1. A clear understanding of individual purposes and goals.
2. A clear understanding of the relationship between these goals and company goals.
3. The consistent application of integrity in all phases of living.
4. The understanding that while the job is part of the whole person, it is just a job unless the whole person applies himself to it.

Drudgery Depends on Attitude

A tendency to view the job as a tedious and necessary evil is primarily caused by the worker's failure to understand its *why*. There are other reasons, of course, but this is by all odds the greatest.

I remember a kiln worker in a brickyard. He approached every Blue Monday with deadly grimness and barely "existed" till the day's work was over and he could enjoy himself. Weekends were all that sustained him. It was clear that he had no pride in his job or his skill, didn't know what the company stood for or where it was going. In his work area, asinine quips were popular. ("You don't have to be crazy to work here, but it helps.") Each man had evolved an attitude that was highly self-centered and defensive—including the need to look as busy as possible the minute the big boss came around.

It was fascinating to watch this particular worker as the temperature of the motivational climate was slowly created. The change did not come overnight—far from it. But ultimately this person began to enjoy his job. The new zest for work put a twinkle back in his eye and a bounce in his walk.

The "Clean Desk" Executive

It has been said here that the climate of an organization can be sensed in fairly short order by the experienced and competent analyst, and that office accoutrements and the general state of work areas are good barometers.

The president of a sizable Midwestern company had a large, bare office. He sat with his back to one corner so that he could survey all sides of his domain. The door to the office had a small one-way window. A subordinate who wanted to come in had to wait until the president pushed a buzzer under the desk and a door would open. As the visitor entered, the desk was always between him and the president.

This man's acumen in business matters was very great. He knew personally how to analyze materials and how to "buy low and sell high." He worked hard, even though suspiciously. His business did not grow, however, and he wondered why. Here was a top executive who would not recognize the value of human warmth and could not be convinced of the need for a change. Some of the negative results were:

1. Poor communication. Since he was remote and hard to approach, he received only the information he demanded. His subordinates' seeming reluctance to cooperate helped make him increasingly uneasy and suspicious.
2. Poor performance. Since the employees were viewed with sus-

picion, there seemed to be no reason why they should extend themselves to please the boss. Innovation was shut off.

3. Poor control. Documents and records alone are inadequate; the best control is enlightened, motivated people who *want* to produce.
4. Poor planning. Without the participation of the people on the firing line, the potential value of short- and long-range planning was short-circuited.

There is much to be said for a physical work atmosphere that lends itself to affability, vulnerability, and stretch. And they are not incompatible. The stretching, sometimes demanding motivational climate usually creates and thrives on affability and warmth. The executive who maintains a clean, arid desk top for appearance's sake often runs an arid department. An effective rule of thumb is: The only reason for documents on the desk is to get something done. If they can accomplish nothing now or in the future, get rid of them.

The Martinet

The martinet seems to feed on the weaknesses of others and often derives a feeling of strength and omnipotence from surrounding himself with weaklings. There is no justification for retaining this kind of person in a management position. In the tough-minded environment, he must change or get out.

The brittle, domineering, and sometimes blustering supervisor or manager who relies on temper, temperament, and invective to run a department or a business is building no warmth or allegiance—nothing permanent or lasting—nothing that will close the ranks behind him when the chips are down. Business foes and political victims are often waiting for a weakening so as to move in fast.

The head of a large shipping department insisted that his employees have no college training and, preferably, not even be high school graduates. He took pains to set up conversational situations which always gave him the last word—usually cryptic or cutting. He also was proud of the fact that everybody was overworked. Some of his people thought he was intelligent, some respected him a little, but most viewed him with amusement, disdain, or disgust.

This department, superficially, had all the signs of a taut ship: the boss was very much in evidence at all times, and his people scurried about busily. However, productivity records in terms of *ac-*

complishment did not stand up well when the methods group began a study of procedures and, shortly afterward, the shipping chief had to go to the hospital for an operation. "*Now* watch that department go to pieces," he told friends.

His temporary replacement was a person of both warmth and firmness. He made it clear to all the employees that each would be held accountable not only for individual results but for the over-all performance of the department—that people who didn't want to operate in this way could get out. At the same time he moved rapidly to give each employee a feeling of identification with the department.

The results were almost startling. Hitherto grumpy and non-cooperative employees began helping each other to do things better. The physical appearance of the department improved markedly; the quality and quantity of work increased dramatically; and, when the "martinet" returned from the hospital, it seemed inconceivable to put him back in charge and he was accordingly transferred. Here was another instance where warmth and insight proved to be essential components of tough-minded management.

It is a common fallacy that the truly great military leaders have been martinets. Yet careful examination will show that while there have been a number of mediocre military officers who were either officious authoritarians or permissive weaklings, there have been many Lees, Eisenhowers, Shoups, and Pershings who used an admirable blend of toughness, wisdom, and warmth to achieve great things. True, the major objectives of war are different from those of business: War calls for the destruction of people and materials through their efficient use; business calls for the *building* of people and materials—also through their efficient use. But to get large numbers of people to work in harmony and productivity is the assignment of any leader, and the extent to which he gets the job done determines his mettle.

The Stuff of Management

James Menzies Black has said the qualities of "executiveship" are ambition, judgment, stamina, organizational and administrative strengths, the ability to plan, and communications skill. In attempting to delineate the essence of management, we might substitute for this list of attributes the simple statement that the executive must know how to plan, organize, execute, coordinate, and control—and it is, of course, essential to have a clearer understanding of these components of the managerial job than many executives currently possess.

But the real "stuff" of management—the underpinning of this book, in fact—is less tangible and less measurable. It is courage, firmness, and candor, yes. Empathy, insight, and other evidences of a feeling for people are requirements too, and it should go without saying that we favor using the latest and most sophisticated management tools if they pay their way. But these are not all.

The elusive quality, trait, or attribute is *wisdom*. Sheer intelligence, eloquence, and erudition may propel a person up through the highly competitive ranks of management, but at about the vice-presidential level they cease to be enough. The orderly and logical use of techniques and data may suffice for operating and staff executives, but the truly broad-gauge man with all-pervasive responsibility and authority needs more. Again—wisdom.

A System of Values

What is wisdom? I have asked this question of many people at all levels of management and have received very different but always interesting answers. I myself believe wisdom to be a quality which must be developed to a substantial extent in the fiery furnace of experience—although quite a number of young people have it. Wisdom must include an understanding of—even develop because of—certain basic facts that are true of all so-called normal people. These basic facts include the following:

1. People differ from one another.
2. People have a need for spiritual guidance and belief.
3. People will usually do the thing that promises benefit to them, but human judgment often errs in determining what actions will yield this result.
4. To savor life you must work hard and toward real accomplishment. Unused iron becomes rusty—stagnant water becomes murky.
5. True happiness comes only through giving to others—of knowledge, of encouragement, of guidance, of constructive criticism, of faith, of some material things.
6. Over the long pull it is impossible to give away more than you receive.

7. Dignity is a way of life, not a convenient façade.
8. Intelligence expressed within a framework of self-interest alone is almost always futile when the end of the story is reached.
9. Untapped potential lies dormant in just about everyone.
10. Sacrificing individual liberty for collective "security" never has produced real happiness.
11. Self-interest is normal and natural but can be fully realized only through and by the development of others.
12. We all have strengths and weaknesses, but concentration in increasing the strengths will usually correct the weaknesses.
13. Education is not a destination but a continuing journey.
14. The highest level of mental hygiene derives from an attitude and feeling of *gratitude*—felt and expressed, spoken and unspoken. Depression and mental illness cannot coexist with it.

The person with wisdom *must* have values. He must have his own idea—workable within the mores of our culture and the world—of what constitutes good and bad, sorrow and joy, moderation and intemperance. He must have appetites, but they must be directed toward positive achievement and must be controlled.

Work Is Life

The keen mind dims without work. The relish of leisure time grows stale. I feel sorry, indeed, for the many who view their work only as something to shuffle through in order to "enjoy" themselves at the end of the day and on weekends. We live in a reasonably enlightened age—but how more unrealistic can such a view be?

A substantial part of our lives is spent in working whether we enjoy it or not. It is certainly the better part of wisdom, then, to try very hard to determine the positives in each job and to maximize them. This can be done to a surprising extent in the motivational climate.

All employees must understand that work is not and cannot be separated from life—work is life, and life is work. Realistically speaking, it is not only the people at the worker level who need to make this transition; a fitting scale of values is needed at the top of the pyramid also. And talent is going to waste at a pitiful rate among our retired population. Let Clarence B. Randall, who has since retired, tell about it:

The saddest part of all for me . . . is the plight of the man who fights retirement for his own sake. "What will I do?" What a commentary on business as a career! "My office is a pretty comfortable place, and I'd be bored to death just sitting around the house. So would my wife." Are the stockholders conducting a social agency for the purpose of solving the inner frustrations of aging officials? "I have no hobby." How I hate that word! As though whittling would solve everything if more widely practiced as an art.

What has such a man been doing all his life? Has nothing challenged him except the daily routine? Has he no unfinished business in terms of the durable satisfactions of life; no dreams that have not come true for which there is still abundant time? Has he never lifted his eyes to the world about him and sensed the infinite variety of opportunity that awaits a man of proven ability for service to his community? Actually, in these critical days when every ounce of energy and every scrap of wisdom could and should be harnessed for the good of our country, and of the world, where is there a comparable reserve of brains and character such as could be provided if every businessman upon retirement would volunteer his service on a full or part time basis, suited to his health, in some form of public activity? It is the pay-off time for the man who has enjoyed the fruits of free enterprise to repay society for extending to him that privilege.[3]

Warmth and Empathy

The pervasive and infectious warmth transmitted by the highly successful person does not spring full-blown from a barren soul.

The physician who has excellent technical accomplishments and credentials but who falls short of total effectiveness and success is relatively common. The minister who has had long years of training and preaching experience but who limits himself to sonorous and pious pronouncements is all too common. Teachers who transmit nothing more than book content to their students are a permanent liability in these days of teacher shortages and overflowing classrooms. And many executives, unfortunately, fall into this same category: They often see their job as one to slog through methodically or as a series of manipulations and machinations.

How is warmth generated and manifested? First, it does *not* mean a perpetual, toothy smile or fatuous and contrived pats on the back.

[3] Clarence B. Randall, *A Creed for Free Enterprise,* Little, Brown and Company (1952), pp. 172–173.

It cannot be achieved by holding periodic performance appraisals. Attempting to bestow "recognition" when the employee knows he doesn't deserve it misses the target utterly and can do more harm than good. Warmth emanates from a person only when he has certain positive beliefs and purposes, and he can transmit this feeling to a subordinate best when they both know what the subordinate is working toward and *why*. Warmth is impossible without empathy. You must be projecting and thinking in terms of the other person's feelings and needs to be truly warm.

The motivational climate engenders these qualities. It provides for the establishment of both personal and job goals for all personnel. It clearly stipulates accountability for failure to measure up. It provides for counsel, for need fulfillment, for rewards commensurate with performance, for freedom of personality, and for a oneness and communality of purpose which will very likely become the management wave of tomorrow.

Warmth is a product of the entire value system presented in this book. It is worth noting that those who try to "for*get*" problems they have had with others rather than "remembering and for*giving*" usually have lifestyles based on "getting" from others. Those tough-minded people who can consistently for*give* usually have lifestyles based on "giving" to others.

Since life is a great cybernetic and we reap precisely what we sow, it is only pragmatic good sense that the more we give—the more we get.

The tough-minded self-actualizer, however, sees through and beyond this kind of petty self-serving. As he or she moves into and through the consecutive stages of self-discovery, self-fulfillment, and self-actualization, this kind of person experiences the zest, the joy, the transcendent pleasure which is available to all those who care enough to truly try.

Most people *want* to be self-actualized, but not enough to *decide* to be.

How about *you?*

15

The forces shaping the world of tomorrow are already in motion.

The Electronic Age:
Problems and Blessings

TECHNOLOGY has advanced further in the past ten years than in all the preceding recorded history of the world. This is almost staggering to comprehend. Many people who definitely do not consider themselves old can remember clearly when the Model-T and the spring wagon were the best available transportation and Americans still held fast to Washington's admonition to avoid "entangling alliances." Yet jet planes, the population explosion, the emergence of new nations in Africa and Asia, the European Economic Community, the astronauts' exploits, and a myriad of other phenomena are marching us inexorably forward. And we in management continue to handle the bulk of our activities in ways best calculated to cope with only yesterday's and today's problems.

The business world of the future can and should be exciting and challenging for the tough-minded manager. It may appear at times to be one never-ending quandary, but with proper planning it need not be.

The Kaleidoscopic Decade

To plan for a productive future in the electronic age, it is important to see where we've been heading the past ten years.

International developments, like technology, have moved with breathtaking speed. The world political climate has initiated new processes which have acted to reweld and remold traditional concepts. The alliance of the Common Market nations has brought about a shift in the economic balance of power; once omnipotent American businesspeople are too often awakening too late to realize that up-and-coming German industries and others have grasped part of their traditional share of the market. Results are being felt from newly built and tooled factories made necessary by the destruction of World War II and made possible by an aroused people who, exposed to U.S. methods and counsel, have seen a way to achieve individual goals in the new economic structure. Automated plants superior to their U.S. counterparts have mushroomed in West Germany particularly; but, more important, the workers and managers in many of these plants are willing to work extraordinarily hard for their wages, by U.S. standards.

Technological changes in this country have occurred at a dizzying rate, with outlays for research and development zooming upward. Factory automation, new-product development, and office mechanization have proceeded side by side. Many of our present computer applications would have been labeled impossible just a few years ago—indeed, the whole concept of computerization was not thought feasible by numerous executives. Yet "electronic data processing," "operations research," "linear programming," "nuclear energy," "transistor," and many other terms which were understood only hazily in the laboratories of the forties have become an essential part of today's business vocabulary, and the use of these sophisticated tools has climbed steadily.

This kaleidoscopic picture has been instrumental in jarring many companies into a sharp awareness of the need for long-range planning. Few, however, have learned how to bring up-to-date management disciplines squarely to bear on this challenge so as to arrive at usable blueprints for action. One notable exception is IBM.

Automation—Servant or Master?

For example, the head of a large tire-manufacturing plant recently told me, "I'd like to shoot the guy who invented the word 'automation.` The term itself has created a real bugaboo, and it's all so unnecessary. Whatever problems are caused by automation are the fault not of the equipment but of the people."

Automation and its uses and misuses in the motivational climate of the future do, to be sure, require careful analysis:

What is automation?
Where can and should it be used?
When should it be used?
Who is involved?
How should it be used?
Why is it important?

The term "automation" simply means automatic operation. In its broader sense, it means production activity through the use of technical equipment—sometimes purely mechanical but, increasingly, electronic. Our principal concern here is the part to be played by automation in the well-managed business of today and tomorrow. For our purposes, then, we shall deal here primarily with the use of electronic data processing (EDP) and integrated data processing (IDP) to enable management to perform more effectively. To put it very simply, what is needed for better management is a better management information system within which EDP and IDP can function.

From coast to coast around the clock, complex hardware is spewing forth hundreds of pounds of data. But much of the time this is *all* it is doing. The key questions, therefore, are these: "What will the data be used for?" and, "Does all this information contribute to achieving the objectives of the department and/or the company?"

Record keeping, bookkeeping, machine accounting have all been vastly refined by the new hardware and systems. Some of the applications are: sales forecasts, cost analysis, payroll procedures, property accounting, inventory control, production control, general ledger accounting, cost accounting, invoicing, budgeting, capital accounting, installment-loans control, stock level control, merchandise control, work-in-process control, accounts receivable analysis, labor-distribution analysis, workload forecasting, traffic management, dividend computations, logistics studies, equipment-performance analysis, comparative costs analysis, shop-load scheduling, shop-order writing.

I have toured companies where the data-processing section was regarded as the highlight of the trip and have listened to the person in charge wax eloquent about the total quantity of data produced. I have asked other executives in the company to tell me the reason for all the hardware. Almost always the answers justify the expense largely on the basis of savings accomplished through the reduction of overhead.

The history of data-processing equipment in business and industry thus far is analogous in many ways to the long, tedious, and often expensive experiences many companies went through in marketing their products before discovering a basic and very simple fact: you produce goods or services to meet reasonably well-known consumer needs, rather than create a product and then wonder how to sell it.

In the majority of companies, incredibly, we are still undergoing these throes in the process of harnessing automation in the form of EDP. It has almost literally become the master in many instances. Why is this? There are several reasons:

1. The complex nature of the equipment and the systems has top management daunted. Executives don't know enough, they feel, to ask probing, penetrating questions.
2. Real control of the systems/data-processing group seldom exists; live, meaningful accountability for profit performance has not been established.
3. The head of the systems/data-processing function is usually a highly trained technician, engineer, or technologist. Entrepreneurial considerations are usually as vague to her as the technical processes are to her boss or her boss's boss.
4. Too often the systems planners view business as a cold, mechanistic, quantifiable process rather than a group of people working toward business objectives—people with human reactions and frailties.
5. The tendency sometimes is to build the department into an electronic empire for individual gain.

The Objective View

Instead of regarding automation as a looming complexity, it is important to see it clearly as only an additional but potentially valuable *resource*. It must be viewed with the same objective detachment applied to any other major new development. Above all, management should not be stampeded into "keeping up with the Joneses." Trite though this may sound, it is happening frequently. The president of a medium-sized department store, for example, was pressured into installing a large computer because his competitors were apparently considering it and he wanted to stay ahead of them. The computer was busy only about 10 percent of the time and lost money steadily. The store's competitors, learning of all this, still proceeded to automate—but with much simpler equipment and systems tailored to their needs.

To make sure that this important resource becomes his servant and not his master, the tough-minded executive will take steps substantially as follows:

1. Staff the top position with a well-rounded person who has administrative insight, who can visualize the contribution of the systems/data-processing group to the entire organization.
2. Clearly define the performance requirements for the function and the person.
3. Make certain that the specific objectives of the systems/data-processing department are realistic, well understood, and designed to contribute directly to company and/or divisional objectives.
4. Evaluate the profit contribution of the EDP unit and see that it is held accountable for total accomplishment. The EDP unit should, of course, be audited; it must not be considered sacrosanct. Many such units have cost data on all the other departments of the business but don't know the cost of their own operation. Worse yet, management often doesn't seem to care.
5. Apply appropriate industrial engineering tools to the flow of data and the design of the system. Ironically, many companies have done this in every department but data-processing. A thorough methods study here can yield real dividends if carried out within the framework of the motivational climate.

As the trend to profit planning and profitability accounting increases, the effect on EDP will be healthy. It must then be justified on the basis of real effectiveness. First, it must make a direct and measurable contribution to more effective planning and control; the data it turns out must have prognostic and projective value. Second, this contribution will be evaluated in the knowledge that automation is best used as a resource, not as an end in itself; that the lofty role coveted by many EDP people is organizationally unhealthy, encouraging them to justify their status by more and more applications dealing with more and more obscure areas of the business. Third, there will be much more knowledgeable *use* of this *resource* by middle management, implemented by realistic performance requirements. Finally, there will be increased emphasis on administrative skill and broad-gauge planning and cooperation on the part of the systems/data-processing manager.

More than ever, the person in management is seen here to grow rather than diminish in importance. The need for new skills, new dimensions of understanding, new values and habits will be increasingly highlighted. The company which becomes a servant to the machine with an accompanying loss of individuality and dignity, will drift into sorry straits indeed. There is not now, nor can we foresee a time when there ever will be, any substitute for human judgment.

The Operations Research Techniques

The use, misuse, and disuse of operations research today illustrate clearly the difficulties of both intracompany and intercompany communication. It is estimated that not over 13 percent of the companies which could benefit from this relatively new tool are now using it. For operations research, first developed in World War II to aid the Allies in solving complex logistical problems, is only *relatively* new.

Definitions of operations research vary widely according to the background and experience of the definer. However, they reduce approximately to this: Operations research employs mathematical tools and concepts within a scientific framework of methodology to evaluate the implications of various courses of action. The major types of operations research may be divided into eight categories: probability theory, symbolic logic, decision theory, queuing theory, linear programming, game theory, information theory, and Monte Carlo techniques.

There has been much discussion concerning the interrelationship of the systems/data-processing people, the operations research people, and the managers of the business. To a considerable extent, it is still the view of many of these people that a chasm yawns between them. There is need for a greater communality of thought, for the mutual solution of semantic problems, and for a united and integrated approach to better management. Instead, we have polite finger pointing. Each group often tends to feel it has the real answer to the company's future success.

Let's reduce this problem to its simplest denominators and see if a problem really exists:

1. Top management needs meaningful, well-organized information in order to make the best decisions possible. Both the systems/data-processing unit and the operations research unit can play a vital role here.
2. Operations research needs meaningful and valid information in order to construct mathematical models or other configurations as appropriate. The analysis and research are only as effective as the information available. The product of the research is made available to management for decision-making purposes, and the basic data are, or can be, obtained from the systems/data-processing unit.
3. The systems/data-processing unit exists to provide services in three general areas:
   a. Information direct to top management and appropriate middle management to implement forward planning and control.
   b. Information to operations research for analysis, synthesis, evaluation, and transmission to decision-level management.
   c. Processing involved in the necessary applications (payroll, general ledger accounting, invoicing, etc.).

We see, then, that the gaps between these parts of the business are often fictional and are caused primarily by self-concern, defensiveness, and empire building. These are in turn often a product of the lack of clear company, departmental, and personal goals or objectives; poor communication; insufficient or inadequate performance requirements; lack of accountability for results; and an atmosphere which fails to stress measurement of the worth of every unit or department strictly in terms of contribution to over-all objectives.

Mathematical Parameters

"Parameters" is a term we hear more and more. Mathematics will almost certainly be used with increasing frequency and versatility during the coming years. It is all the more important, therefore, that we develop a conceptual or administrative framework which will make mathematical techniques of maximum value.

So it is, too, with PERT and critical path techniques. Their potential value in planning and control can be great indeed if they are viewed simply as powerful tools or resources and used within an enlightened administrative climate.

A tendency still exists to apply the disciplined approach inherent in mathematical computations to the entire range of business problems—and this may be all very well, if properly done. It does, however, mean using mathematical guidelines or parameters for stretch and growth rather than in an overly precise and restrictive manner.

I might cite as an example of what not to do the case of a chief engineer who was once sent to me for counsel. His superior, also an engineer, called at 9:00 a.m. and said, "Please teach him human relations quickly because he has a meeting at 10:30." During the counseling session which followed, I made a real attempt to break through the chief engineer's icy detachment and to develop in him some real understanding of how to stimulate and lead people. He made scrupulous notes and, at exactly 10:25, rose and said in effect, "Now I'm all set. I've mastered the principles of human relations." I pointed out that this was a little premature, but he retorted, "Either a thing works or it doesn't—and there's no reason why these principles shouldn't work."

Some days later I visited this person's department and found an atmosphere of low morale and semi-hostility. Upon investigation, I found that he walked from one person to another each morning and mechanically inquired about the health of wives and children, checked off each name on his pad, and moved on. This quantitative application of qualitative matters to a department composed of diverse and variable human beings was downright detrimental. The situation was corrected only when the chief engineer saw clearly that empathy, warmth, understanding, perception, and even hunch and intuition have an important role in management.

The cyclical fluctuation in the popularity of psychological tests is another case in point. They can be valuable if properly used, but some years ago they were oversold and a period of disenchantment followed. In recent years, new and better tests have been constructed, and now it is generally accepted that they can be useful tools *if properly used.* They simply must not be thought of as a whole administrative way of life.

These cases have been mentioned because the pattern which they reflect may be closely related to the new enthusiasm and eagerness in some quarters to solve the problems of management by overreliance on mathematics and other quantitative methodology.

It is not enough to arrange a group of outstanding musicians in an orchestra and tell them to play a certain score, even though the mathematically correct number of instruments is there. It is still not enough to distribute music which each has played individually before. Again, this meets the quantitative requirements only. What is needed is a leader who knows what total effect is wanted, who knows how to communicate this to each player, who can explain what each must contribute, who can help the group *want* to play well and can evaluate both total musical effect and individual proficiency. Only in this way can there be assurance of blended, harmonious accomplishment, of subtle shadings in tone and pitch.

The same thing is obviously true of a department or of a company. And the more sophisticated the quantity and quality of the instruments become the greater is the need for leadership or management skill. Whether it is an orchestra or a machining or credit department, the best way to achieve end results is to determine what they should be and then develop a climate to achieve them.

Organizational Impact

There is a considerable movement under way which favors the establishment of fairly massive central offices labeled variously as management or administrative services. These are almost wholly staff services. In a great many instances, companies are becoming topheavy with planners, researchers, and advisers without really knowing why. Coordinators and assistants are springing up rapidly.

The tough-minded manager must recognize that many of the deep vertical organization charts will have to flatten out; otherwise, disenchantment with the whole idea of centralized services and integrated data processing may be inevitable. The executive who wants to steer a taut ship wants these innovations to pay for themselves.

As L. C. Guest, Jr., former vice president-administration of the General Telephone and Electronics Corporation, has said:

Management wants data processing to function in a business-like manner. Those engaged in this activity are increasingly vocal in their insistence that they should be considered members of the management team within their respective companies. Fine! If they will assume the prerogatives of management, they must also assume the responsibilities of management. They must, therefore, make a real and measurable contribution to the company's profit position and protect its share-of-market position and competitive strength.

They must program their activities with a greater degree of accuracy and meet promised work schedules and project-completion dates. They must be more specific in describing the intent and ob-

jectives of systems programs and be able to report the results of
their efforts in terms comprehensible to all. . . . In short, management wants its money's worth.*

The age of electronics is no longer in its infancy but rather is
some three decades old. Many predicted vivid Orwellian nightmares,
wherein the computer became "big brother" and humanism suc-
cumbed first to science and then to scien*tism*.

Happily, this has not happened. What we are seeing in reality is
an accelerating awareness of people, their significance, wants, needs
and problems. Social awareness and individuality are increasingly
becoming recognized as quintessential in actualizing the four freedoms implicit in our free enterprise system. They are freedom of
social, political, economic, and spiritual enterprise.

*In James D. Gallagher, *Management Information Systems and the Computer*, AMA
Research Study 51 (1961), p. 21.

16

Tough-minded management is needed as never before in our history as a nation.

The Free Enterprise Way

THROUGHOUT the world, the struggle for the minds of individuals and for whole cultures and societies is going on relentlessly. The very foundations of our way of life have been challenged. The former leader of the Soviet Union said, "We will bury you." And too often in recent years we have been torn by agonizing self-doubts and confusion.

In essence, we are looking at a clash between collectivism and individualism. The ideological, political, economic, and social outgrowths of this clash are many and diverse; but, fundamentally, it is the individual dignity of man versus the faceless conformity of the collectivists.

Can the Soviet system match our proven democratic system?

The tremendous know-how and determination which we displayed in rallying after Pearl Harbor were an example for the whole world. But we had the advantage then of a central rallying point— we were in danger and knew it. Our varying purposes and goals were quickly fused into one tremendous resolve. Now, however, many complacent overfed and underworked people show no real readiness to face up to a threat that is every bit as real and menacing as the enemy in that war and other wars.

We can narrow our focus, therefore, to the statement that the root of the problem lies in *attitudes*.

Ideas That Build and Strengthen

We said in Chapter 1 that weak spots do exist in our rich and opulent society:

A tendency to confuse hardness with toughness.
Defensive, implosive, and insular attitudes.
Idolization of abrasiveness rather than real strength.
The worship of leisure.
The deification of recreation and amusement.
The pursuit of financial security.
Fear of innovation unless it provides immediate returns in money or leisure.
The loss of tough-minded individuality.
Refuge in mass thinking and collective movements: sheeplike behavior.
A tendency to talk rather than act.
Lack of awareness of our own history.
Failure to take a strong stand for individual beliefs.
A tendency to view the future with trepidation.
Policies reflecting what we are *against* rather than *for*.
Spiritual bankruptcy.

Pervading most of these weaknesses is a desire to get "something for nothing." The tough-minded executive is in an excellent position to blast this sort of thinking with a motivational climate.

New nations are emerging. New millions of people are developing an awareness of and an appetite for the material things of life which we have so long taken for granted. The Soviets are using "gut logic" to appeal to these developing nations; they are saying that their system is better than ours at filling the bellies of hungry people. The resourcefulness and ability of our business organizations, within our free enterprise system, are still more than a match for them, but they are improving and we must too. Only through high productivity can we make and sell goods in world markets at both a reasonable profit to us and a reasonable price for them. At the present time, thanks to narrow thinking on the part of both management and unions, our costs are too high—as everyone knows—in proportion to output.

The motivational climate contributes both directly and indirectly to positive global goals by—

1. Helping employees to build positive, results-oriented attitudes toward their work.
2. Relating their goals to the company's goals.
3. Helping to insure that the company's goals are in consonance with our national purpose.
4. Giving people something to be *for*.
5. Providing more products at more competitive prices to stimulate more buying—and so on, full circle.
6. Providing more jobs and greater income which will result, for instance, in the more general purchase of stock. The broader the base of a private enterprise business, the greater the stability of the whole economy.
7. Earning more profit for more plants—including, in some instances, plants in foreign countries.
8. Encouraging individuality.
9. Recognizing the value and, literally, the life-preserving elements of hard work in an environment of enlightenment and motivation.
10. A pervasive emphasis on integrity.

Harry A. Bullis has said:

> The American scale of living in the future will depend to an important degree on the amount of capital per worker that continues to be invested in American industry. Our economy has been able to remain strong because our system has produced a marked step-up in the rate of capital formation, making possible an equivalent expansion of investment. The amount of money industry invests in tools and equipment for each worker directly affects his productivity. And as each worker's productivity increases, cost per unit decreases, demand grows and consumption is stimulated, new jobs are created and the over-all standard of living rises.

> Thus the process that has brought such great abundance in America begins when business invests capital; then industry can produce and distribute more goods to consumers. If an automobile manufacturer, for instance, wishes to make more cars—more than the capacity of his present facilities—he must build an additional

plant, buy machines, train more workers, and gather inventories of needed materials. Only then can he begin to produce the extra automobiles.[1]

What could be more challenging to tough-minded managers than to exemplify such ideas that build and strengthen? We need to find bigger and better ways to remind our fellow citizens that the history of our country is a great one, and that its future is limited only by the capacity of its people to grow and change. We must somehow get it across that giving of self is the real key to increased productivity and its rewards; that self-pity, self-concern, and bullying are just the reverse of toughness. They are ideas and actions that tear down and weaken.

We must make it clear by our everyday actions and reactions that we believe in the dignity of the individual and that the positive approach is not a catch phrase or a passing fad but a vital way of life. It is amazing how little this is really understood by the bulk of the employees in the average company. The process of encouraging each one to determine what he is most concerned about as a person and what he really wants from life, and of clearly explaining the relationship between these and the goals of the department and company, is not easy. But then, as we have said repeatedly, the easy way isn't always the best way, and the tough-minded man is dedicated to the best.

The Sterility of Materialism

Material fulfillment is normally considered complete when a person's basic appetites are satisfied and there is some surplus. For generations the opponents of free enterprise have had much fodder for their propaganda mills primarily because the great percentage of human beings in the world simply haven't had all their material desires fulfilled. The person who subsists on crusts while others eat sirloin doesn't usually give much thought to spiritual values. He wants some meat first. The person who must walk while others have automobiles is often ripe for materialist propaganda. But there have already been many examples in foreign countries of a continuing hunger and thirst for something *after the material needs are met.*

It is manifest, then, that free enterprise will fulfill one of its

[1] Harry A. Bullis, *Manifesto for Americans,* McGraw-Hill Book Company (1961), pp. 31–32.

greatest purposes when it shows the world what American determination and productivity can do to meet material needs, not only better than communism but because, not in spite, of our human values and beliefs. To state it another way—the harnessed and directed use of the resources of an enlightened and motivated democracy can win the ideological struggle. If we fail to develop this kind of productivity, we shall be in great peril.

A Better Job of Selling

A business which sells its product overseas has a weighty obligation. It places the output of a free democratic society right in the midst of people who know nothing of free enterprise. It is in a very real sense on trial. Its people can be unproductive, churlish, and tactless; its management can be mediocre; or the company can be a tremendous force for democracy and profit in that order.

Mr. Bullis points out:

> We Americans possess enormous strength. Every worthy struggle and every good action of man rise from a spiritual base: the good for which he strives, the service for which he lives. In the American concept of dignity and freedom, in our belief in the divine right of each individual to grow to his full potential and to develop his God-given capacities, we have a compass that can show us—and the world—the way. We can demonstrate that our sustained and constructive effort of economic assistance has for its goal not the exploitation of under-developed peoples, but the development of their own potentialities for their own good.

But the bald fact is that the majority of people throughout the world still do not know what really makes our democracy tick. The elements are not clearly defined and precisely parceled mores, folkways, or laws; they are all part of a mix of blended individualities whose push, pull, and stretch have carved whole new dimensions of business operation. How can we help the rest of the world see what our way of life can mean?

First, we must gain a better knowledge of the forces, drives, and fundamental beliefs that have made us so productive in the past. Next, we must sell the benefits and values of democracy. Selling is American. This is not to say that it is unique to America—Columbus had to do a real job of selling Queen Isabella. But the ingenious merchandising of products and services has been a mighty force in our industrial growth, and we just haven't done a real job of selling what made it all possible—our free enterprise way.

The same tough-minded principles needed to sell ideas in the motivational climate will work. And the really significant achievements in our past have always been the product of tough-minded action. The Boston Tea Party is an outstanding example. This was not a case of apologetically approaching the British; it was planned, decisive follow-through of belief in certain ideals.

The Soviets are doing a better selling job than we in many corners of the world arena. Why? Because the average Communist has been carefully saturated with the Party's objectives. Few foreign commercial representatives of the Russian government would be caught flatfooted if asked to state what they stand for. On the contrary, the average American usually cannot do this. Ours is literally an embarrassment of riches; yet, while we struggle with problems of food surplus made possible by our system, we are depicted in foreign countries as bloated sweatshop operators. We are not getting mileage out of our talents on a worldwide basis—in fact, they are too often liabilities.

The challenges implicit in this situation for the tough-minded executive are relatively simple:

1. To sell, you must know your product. Hence the best way to prepare your company for this biggest of selling tasks, whether it is presently international or not, is to make sure all your employees know the *what, where, when, who, how,* and *why* of their jobs.
2. Then you must make sure the appropriate employees see the "big picture," that they see the benefits to them, as well as their company and their country, of telling what they as individuals stand for and what their company stands for. Here is real, down-to-earth bedrock selling, and it needn't be difficult. The orderly establishment of the motivational climate helps build purpose, direction, and motivation into all employees, equipping them to sell democracy and at the same time make a far greater contribution to a thriving company than representatives of sterile materialism.

In many of the emerging countries we can change from a policy of giving three loaves of bread to a policy of selling one and teaching how to produce the other two. Thus we offer their developing economies a much more lasting and significant form of help while, simultaneously, we build potential markets and buying power for other products.

Talk About Profit

It would be difficult to explain to a visitor from another planet why anything needs to be said about profit. Its importance should be obvious: without profit, our whole abundant way of life would wither away rapidly into a muddled, purposeless sort of socialism. Everybody would have an equal share of nothing but a bare materialist-type subsistence.

I have noticed with increasing chagrin that the word "profit" is being used less and less. The owner of a medium-sized company, for example, badly needed to make certain general repairs in his plant and to buy some new equipment. But, if he did, the union would immediately accuse him of making a profit, saying that an employer who could afford such expense could afford to boost hourly rates. Here was a man who was literally afraid to talk profit.

In this almost completely negative and defensive climate, simply pointing out that without profit there would ultimately be no jobs was not sufficient. It was necessary to start at bedrock and build a whole new appreciation of our free enterprise system. Basic economics, basic politics, and basic facts of life were in order. Severely dated union and management *attitudes* had to be overhauled. Only when these were changed could further steps be taken in the way of new policies, new procedures, new organizational structure, new union contract, new selling methods.

Somewhere and somehow a lot of the people in our country today have gradually become apathetic and even apologetic or defensive about the free enterprise way. The tough-minded manager has his work cut out for him in meeting this challenge, and it can't be met solely by uttering righteous, pontifical phrases through mass communications media. The fires must be lit on many fronts by many people. The tough-minded person knows and exemplifies the kind of thinking and doing that have made us great. He knows, further, that we can't retain and build on this foundation by wishful thinking.

It is amazing how often the biblical question "Am I my brother's keeper?" has been twisted and distorted to mean something like "I *am* my brother's keeper and will continue to be even though he may become or is already capable of keeping himself."

I believe it is healthy to remind such interpreters that the word "work" appears some 687 times in the Bible. I suggest we consider the following as an aphorism for the 1980s:

> *I am not my brother's keeper unless he cannot keep himself. BUT—*
> *I would like to be my BROTHER'S BROTHER and help him KEEP HIMSELF.*

To keep another when he can keep himself is to denigrate him—to help suffocate and stifle his selfhood.

To help a person acquire the strength, confidence, skills, or insights needed to keep himself or herself is to help that person grow in dignity and self-esteem. It is well to ponder whether this kind of mature interpretation could have prevented much of the Vietnam tragedy. Billions for education, agronomy, and other self-help aids might have prevented "billions for destruction." From symptoms to root causes.

What would happen if the United States were to elect a truly tough-minded President?

17

The management statesman relates his philosophy to the entire world around him.

Management in the World Arena

A CALL for management statesmen has been sounded. Our country has the talent, and we are becoming increasingly aware of the need throughout the world.

One can almost hear executives in small and medium-size companies saying, "I don't have time to be a management statesman—I'm too busy running a business. Leave that to the big ones who have lots of staff and lots of time." But the type of manager who conducts himself and his business in a statesmanlike manner needn't spend a lot of time in Washington or overseas.

Multiple Obligations

Who is a management statesman? He or she is the one who sees the big picture, who weighs and assesses the alternatives, and who conditions his or her actions with both wisdom and a tough-minded drive toward positive objectives.

To qualify as a business statesman it is necessary to determine, as a part of your total philosophy, your obligations to and your plans for stockholders, employees, government, consumers, competitors, and the public.

Stockholders have long been effective arbiters in many well-managed companies; in others their influence has been negligible. It is healthy for the top operating executive to be accountable for his performance, and the tough-minded manager does not find this accountability difficult or unpalatable. He knows that a versatile and informed group of stockholders is another resource available to him, and he makes appropriate use of this resource to achieve objectives for their benefit. Stockholder relations have been undergoing great changes: annual reports are more and more readable, jet travel encourages greater attendance, and closed-circuit television is a real aid to effective meetings with groups dispersed over wide geographic areas.

The tough-minded manager needs to establish an orderly and organized procedure for obtaining the best current thinking of all stockholders. One sequence of activities which can be of great aid to the larger firm is as follows:

1. Develop a simple instrument which, in completed form, will lend itself to computer or tabulator programming (punch cards, mark-sense cards, etc.).
2. Send this document or instrument to stockholders at preplanned and coordinated intervals.
3. Program the feedback into appropriate EDP or mechanical equipment to obtain preplanned and categorized information.
4. Utilize the information in conjunction with consumer research and other external conditioning factors for the establishment and/or modification of company objectives.

Dangers lurk here. The top executive—if not tough-minded—may be overly influenced by the stockholders and may follow the course of least resistance rather than one dictated by wisdom and maximum accomplishment. However, if this four-step scheme is properly administered, it provides broad, diversified information for planning and, to some extent, operating purposes; a feeling of identification and participation on the part of stockholders; a sensitive indicator of current attitudes; and coordination at low cost. It does require that the chief operating executive be his own man: he must still call his shots as he sees them, and the stockholders must realize he must.

It is simply the better part of wisdom to learn the attitudes and opinions of stockholders; they exist, after all, whether you know what they are or not. So do the attitudes and opinions of your *employees*—and the employees of an organization are its most precious resource. What does the management statesman do about them? Answers to this question occupy much space in this book but may be summed up succinctly in these words: The development of common men into uncommon men—the expansion and liberation of talents and abilities—challenging and focusing abilities toward the achievement of new dimensions of honorable business and personal accomplishment—this is statesmanship in business.

In relations with *government,* the tough-minded executive is not pliant and permissive or given to carping and sniping. He views government as a necessary and valued bulwark in guarding and perpetuating our system of free enterprise. He proceeds on this positive premise even though his nerves may become ragged on occasion and bureaucracy may appear rampant. It is indeed vital that he continue to do so.

Business gains nothing by simply complaining. It can gain much by exemplifying the principles of tough-minded management on a community, national, and international basis. Government will probably remain big and pervasive for many years whether it is desirable or not. Retreat by business is not the answer. The answer lies in wholehearted cooperation—but cooperation toward more precisely defined goals. Business statesmen must meet more frequently with the heads of government and must vigorously and objectively point out the tremendous potential role of business in the developing countries. Business has certain advantages over government in stimulating international cooperation and good will, but clear ground rules are a "must."

The management statesman views the *consumer* with respect and curiosity. He knows the consumer can make or break him and knows further that we are just beginning to tap the wells of knowledge concerning consumer habits. Market research is emerging from its bog of preoccupation with gimmicks and statistics and is seeking to learn more about the fundamentals of human behavior. Motivation research will continue to move forward on surer ground, but management should increasingly require evidence of its soundness and value.

The *competitor* should be viewed more and more in a new dimension, not as a bogeyman or a prince of evil that will go away if he is not discussed or recognized nor, obviously, as a ripe subject for collusion, price fixing, or other actions which corrode the freedom of both producers and consumers. He must be regarded as a *challenge;* information about one's competitor can stimulate a tremendous force within the motivational climate. This, of course, cannot be merely an occasional thing. It can and must come because every employee sees as part of his greater purpose the besting of the competition from both a quality and a price standpoint.

The management statesman recognizes that the *general public* is an unpredictable and imprecise element in business, but knows that people's attitudes and habits can almost always be distinct assets if he practices management by integrity. In most companies the pendulum has swung wildly at times so far as relations with the public are concerned, as well as with stockholders, employees, government, consumers, and competitors. The optimum has probably never yet been achieved. Certainly, pure reliance upon costly public relations and packaged benefit programs is not for the tough-minded management statesman. Contrary to much popular belief, you cannot buy good will—it is earned in other ways.

Our Resurgent Allies

In the world arena, as we have seen, this country's most pressing consideration is productivity. For many years we enjoyed a unique position largely because of our mastery of mass production. This is no longer true: the developing nations have been busily growing and importing such know-how. Moreover, another diminishing asset is our supply of raw materials, for we no longer lead the world in this respect.

Western Europe and Japan are enjoying a kind of industrial resurgence and prosperity which they have never before experienced. Not so startlingly, one of the biggest reasons for this upsurge is that they are practicing free enterprise and democracy in a way very similar to our own during the most vigorous periods of our industrial history. There is a strong and charged current of belief in the future. In order to maintain and improve on our position in the world's markets, it is vital that we generate too a new kind of belief that "the difficult we do today—the impossible takes a little longer."

The real breakthroughs in management in the world of tomorrow must lie in new methods of motivating people. Increasingly, we will see a balance in technology, physical resources, and material living. The country that has the most people who *want* to work because they know *why* they are working will produce the leaders of tomorrow. Our tendency to emphasize the *how* of working has paid dividends, but this approach has always been incomplete and will be inadequate in the face of emerging worldwide needs.

The Common Market

The rise of the European Common Market promises to be the single most important economic development since the Industrial Revolution. While its formation has been compared to the dropping of trade barriers among the British colonies in North America which eventually led to union and independence in the eighteenth century, it has even greater significance: It has clearly shown that people of diverse social, cultural, economic, and political backgrounds can and will cooperate to meet common goals.

Just as the growth and development of the United States were contingent upon free trade, the Common Market can provide the catalyst and impetus for the economic growth of the West. It would be naïve to limit our thinking to Western Europe alone; the impact of this new revolution must expand to include the whole world, or at least the non-Communist world. Western Europe, Great Britain, and the United States have a total population of half a billion people, while there are over two billion more in the underdeveloped nations of the world. To be truly effective, the members of the Common Market must find a way to bring these nations into the fold and use every resource to speed their development and growth. They must experience the fruits of free enterprise and feel the impact of incentive profit upon their economies to truly understand the benefits of the capitalistic system.

The development of free trade throughout the world will be slow and arduous. Despite its many benefits, it will cause many difficulties and challenge business to the utmost. One of the greatest problems for today's manager will be the need to anticipate change and prepare for the future rather than fight it. Even in areas that now seem provincial, he must start thinking internationally, looking at the American market as just one of many. Foreign trade can no longer be a marginal activity of the American business. Expanding international markets must be developed not only for their own sake but to compete effectively on the domestic scene.

In short, while the opportunities are tremendous, the Common Market will further accentuate the need for tough-minded management in American business. Common Market countries, by exploiting American markets, are going to create one of the most competitive situations in our history. With a minimum differential of one dollar in hourly wage rates between United States and Europe, it will take all the ingenuity management can muster to meet this competitive threat. But it is this type of competition that can make America even stronger economically as management is forced to become tougher-minded, to create the motivational climate, to seek new dimensions of marketing innovation, to cut production costs still further, and to use every ounce of available creativity and imagination in the task.

The Disciplined Executive

The disciplined mind is the reverse of the dogmatic mind. A constant hunger for new knowledge, new experiences, and new achievements is the mark of the disciplined executive. And such discipline is imperative for the tough-minded executive in the world arena.

Retreat, anxiety, and suspicion are products of the loosely organized person who builds up a record of abortive experiences. He often does this because he is operating in a sterile management vacuum. The components of the business are compartmentalized "areas" of functional activity whose principal objective often is just to keep busy. There are whole organizations—even whole communities and states—whose attitude seems to be that sporadic studies, projects, and "efforts" will bring about growth and prosperity. This just doesn't work out.

Someone must assume both authority and accountability for putting together an organized, cohesive total effort made up of individuals who are truly individuals. And, although every successful effort calls for strong individualism, those people must be convinced of the value of the broad objectives at stake and clearly see what they will be required to accomplish.

The kind of executive who can breathe the necessary spirit into a company or community must be big—he must have purpose, courage, and wisdom. He must relate his own philosophy to the entire world around him but must exercise sufficient discipline of mind to insist on top performance from everyone involved.

On the international scene, our use of the phrase "human rights" is receiving much attention. The tough-minded manager knows that the *example* of our businesses, government, educators, and individuals will speak most loudly throughout the world.

18

Rights are ours only if we qualify to maintain them.

Above All, Integrity

IF we seek to set forth the present and future role of the tough-minded executive, it is not enough simply to recount the part which business has played in helping the free enterprise system yield a high standard of living for the nation. For the facts and trends clearly indicate that business at present does not enjoy the status it once had. Great inroads into its freedom of action have been made by (1) big government and (2) labor unions.

What has happened? If an entrepreneur starts a business and builds it with his or her own blood, sweat, and tears, why can't it be within a general framework of law? Or, in the case of the publicly owned corporation, why hasn't management the "right" to function without undue interference by government? These are good questions and must be answered.

The salient point here is that "rights" are rights only if we earn them. They are, in a very real sense, only privileges. We in management have lost some measure of our rights by not qualifying to retain them.

Free Enterprise for All

First, let's examine what has happened inside the company to affect management's position negatively.

In the years to come, management will increasingly realize the dated role it is playing when it presumes to solve employees' problems *for* them instead of *with* them. This in no way implies co-determination. It does mean, however, that the latent forces in every employee cannot be molded into neat, comfortable cells of conformity without trouble.

The problems of conformity which have reduced whole societies to awkward aimlessness are rearing their heads in the smothering "organization man" climate of many contemporary companies. As James C. Worthy says:

> One of the ironies of modern times is the failure to see the full implications of the free enterprise system for the internal conduct of business affairs. Business eagerly defends the free economic process against the stifling effects of too much government control, but often fails to see that the essential principles advocated for government apply equally to the organization and administration of business, and that the violation of these principles produces within business itself the same stifling results, the same frustration of spontaneous productive energy, that their violation in the larger field of government policy produces within the general economic system.
>
> Perhaps the greatest challenge of modern times is for creative business leadership which can develop within industry itself the methods of democratic organization and control which have been worked out for the political state. Obviously, this is no easy task. Political institutions cannot be taken over intact by business. Business cannot be run by a ballot box or by a Congress. We must develop other inventions, adapted to the special circumstances of business, which will give to employees at all levels of our economic organization a greater sense of personal participation, a greater sense of belonging, a greater sense of dignity and recognition for their worth as individuals and as respected members of the industrial community.[1]

An organization of enlightened individuals who are working toward clearly defined company and personal goals will always excel over those companies which are ramrodded by a few people who are too small to realize what they are doing to themselves, their businesses, and the free enterprise way. For free enterprise applies to *all*.

A direct outgrowth of the failure to realize and practice this fun-

[1] James C. Worthy, *Big Business and Free Men*, Harper & Row (1959), pp. 55–56.

damental truth is the rise of unions. We do not introduce the motivational climate with any thought of eliminating unions, though it can certainly help insure that they are restricted to their rightful role. We may properly say, however, that in the true motivational climate unionization should largely be unnecessary in that collective representation with emphasis on seniority is not as effective as the realization of personal goals through greater productivity—reward for results, not activity.

Which brings us to the matter of integrity.

A Working Definition

Integrity does not lend itself to compromise. It is not gray, it is either all black or all white. It must not be worn on one's sleeve but must be a way of life. Perhaps the following definition will be of help: *Integrity is that quality of a man or woman which requires that the only real purpose of any thought, word, or deed be to build persons or things, in order to accomplish positive and ethical results.* This is difficult and perhaps unrealistic for many of us now. But we are not just talking about now—we are focusing on a future way of business life that must show the way to the rest of the world.

Can holes be punched in this definition by the cynic, the despot, the negative intellectual? I have issued this challenge many times and have never seen it effectively answered. In reality, isn't the whole reason for business to *build things,* to *sell* them, to *satisfy* needs? Negative action, negative planning, negative controls, negative motivation—try these deliberately and watch your department or company stall and start backward.

Integrity Must Be Pervasive

John C. Bosted of the National Association of Manufacturers says that "free enterprise is first of all a system of morality." And a system—by definition—is a pervasive thing that reaches into many recesses of the business.

I have examined the findings of countless employee attitude surveys and have studied the answers to open-end questions by the hour. Many top executives, as well as middle management personnel, should do this. They might be surprised to find that hourly-paid employees seldom use the word "integrity" per se. Most workers know what it means, and many of them live the way it implies, but often the same people are oblivious to speeches and printed material which pompously espouse it.

The average worker has a much better understanding of integrity when he sees it practiced by his boss and his boss's boss—when he can be proud of what he reads in the papers about the company. The motivational climate helps insure this by stressing integrity from the grass roots up. It—

1. Places greater emphasis on positive values and beliefs during the screening process before a new employee is hired.
2. Stresses these same values and beliefs throughout the orientation process.
3. Builds them into the performance requirements for each position and person.
4. Reflects them in communications media on a continuous basis—not just a feature article now and then.
5. Accepts nothing less than candor—but candor which is warm and motivated by a sincere desire to build up rather than tear down.
6. Holds all personnel accountable for applied honesty.

Growth of a Business Conscience

The efforts of business to proclaim its integrity and the values of free enterprise have been caustically dissected by many critics. These self-styled authorities are effective in pointing out the weaknesses of business, but they too often neglect to say what should be done about them. We see far too much of this just about everywhere we look.

More harm than good is done when we enumerate all the ways in which business is falling down in its many obligations and fail utterly to cite the abundant contributions it has made to society economically, socially, politically, and morally. Not that we would want to white-wash business in general. Referring back to the growth of unions, we say again that management wrongs were in many cases responsible. However, these wrongs included various types of exploitation that, fortunately, now are things of the past. Many well-administered unions played a healthy catalytic role in the reformation of those businessmen who countenanced intolerable situations. (Others, less happily, used them to set up parasitic operations.) The important thing is that widespread exploitation is no more and a new and genuine business conscience has been growing.

Whether or not it can be justified, the insidious extension of government control and interference in business can—to a certain degree, at least—be explained. The prime offense of business has, of course, been in the general category of monopolistic practices. Much remains to be done before business will be in a completely defensible position in this respect. Considerably more should be done to bring about agreement on definitive codes of ethics in certain industries, and these codes should be made clear to the general public, with particular emphasis on stockholders. When stockholders are poorly informed about the *why*'s of major management decisions, they are likely to exert pressures for moves which are not in the best interest of the company.

Many of the same businesspeople who tell their children that two wrongs don't make a right justify certain practices, such as price fixing, by saying they do it only because others do. The tough-minded executive, however, is a conscience-guided trend maker, not a blind follower and conformer.

Why Integrity Is Natural

It is sometimes argued that integrity is not natural, that it is an artificial restraint placed on societies to enable people to live together in relative harmony. This point of view would suggest further that laws are not natural, and accordingly we can always count on a large number of lawbreakers.

To see clearly that integrity is not only a desirable but a very natural way of life, we must examine some deeply entrenched myths.

1. That everybody looks out for himself first.
2. That one's human needs are better met by getting than giving.
3. That self-discipline is necessary to control negative drives rather than to implement positive ones.

It is well known that children claw and fight to get things from others at certain ages. But, as time goes by, they become more thoughtful and courteous—not only because they fear discipline or punishment but, to a much greater extent, because they realize there is a certain intrinsic pleasure to *them* in the act of giving. The truly wise person knows that the great secret of fulfillment in any walk of life is to *get out of himself* and help others.

Our great challenge, then, is to find better ways to communicate this fundamental truth to enough people. It is difficult for many to comprehend, largely because it is so simple and obvious. Must there be a more complex and esoteric explanation of why to practice integrity, of how to be successful? Not at all.

"The Young Sophisticate"

A man in his late thirties was telling me about his job dilemma. His education and experience were excellent; his personal appearance and grooming were impeccable; he talked rapidly and persuasively. He had been interviewed by the presidents of some of the best-managed firms in the country; and, although he had reviewed his performance in these interviews many times, he couldn't determine what was wrong. The net result, however, was clear: he had not yet been offered a job at the level to which he aspired.

The key to his problem was his emphasis on the word "sophisticated" throughout his conversation with me. It was clear that he had been putting on an act during each interview, that he was trying to do all the "sophisticated" and "correct" things he had read about in books. The thing he was not doing was to demonstrate the most vital ingredient in any position and particularly a high one. *He was not being himself.*

When the enlightened top executive selects an assistant or promotes a person into a responsible position, he must be able to rely on that person above all else. The knowledge that the subordinate will meet commitments in spite of obstacles, that he will steer clear of internal politics, that his word is solid, is central to any position of real trust. It follows, therefore, that whoever presents an artificial veneer of sophistication—whoever does not seek to sell himself on his real merits—is unrealistic, lacking in judgment, and insincere. And realism, judgment, and sincerity all are qualities one must have to merit hire or promotion in the well-managed company.

This young man quit acting like a stereotyped "smart young comer" and began first to build a new results-oriented approach into the job he then held. Some time later he again began his job search and concentrated not on his personal background but on what he could accomplish for his prospective employer. Not only did he find new doors open to him, but his employer offered him a raise and a promotion to remain.

The mature reader can recall similar situations. These are down-to-earth bread-and-butter illustrations of integrity in action. There is no alternative that has stood the test of time.

"The Old Smoothie"

The middle years can and should be a time for the executive to indulge in some pretty pleasant reflections about what has been accomplished thus far. We see two extreme types of executives in this stage of their careers, often at middle-management levels.

One is the person who becomes increasingly cynical and fearful as he grows older. He feels strongly that others, particularly better-educated people, may be out to get his job or undermine him in some way. He becomes increasingly withdrawn or overtly aggressive. In either case he usually doesn't contribute much to his own sense of accomplishment or to that of others. Almost invariably he stresses activity in his work rather than results. He can often tell you eloquently about what he is working at rather than what he is getting done. He is the "realist," the negativist, the fussbudget.

At the other end of the continuum is the person who has learned that the solution to market slumps, production bottlenecks, and automation problems is seldom a new system or procedure but rather the development of people. He may be a chief research chemist, a controller, or a general supervisor. He is not necessarily trained in psychology or personnel management; more often he is the person who has built and crossed the bridge from mere intelligence to the more elusive quality known as wisdom, which has as its postulate the development of others. The latter years for the man who has developed real pleasure and skill in helping others to grow can be mellow indeed. He knows his life exemplifies *building*—not destruction.

"The old smoothie" is usually somewhere between these two extremes. He enjoys making people feel good—but only if he can do so without any inconvenience or travail to himself. He stresses affability and is adept as a soother. He usually has not made the full transition necessary to become a topnotch tough-minded manager, for the tough-minded person must have the guts to put himself to some emotional inconvenience for the sake of getting through artificial defense mechanisms and getting real growth started.

For instance, the marketing vice president who knows his sales manager is getting into deep water through some extramarital involvement may find it painful or embarrassing—if he is an old smoothie—to sit down and talk the situation over. It may seem easier to evade the matter and mentally resolve to fire the man if he doesn't get squared away. But if this vice president is tough-minded, if he practices integrity, he will face this situation that threatens the sales manager. In the process, both will grow and the company will benefit as well.

The old smoothie may be nice to talk to at a party, but he will become a better executive when he gets more steel in his backbone, when he learns to practice integrity.

Ramifications of Management Decisions

It is needless to point out ad infinitum that the world is growing smaller, moving faster, becoming more complex. It is important, however, to point up the wide and diverse effects of integrity and its presence, or absence, on the firing line of business.

Only a few years ago, the ramifications of decisions to raise prices, modernize packaging, diversify product lines, grant raises to bargaining-unit personnel, or realign distribution channels were often felt only in the United States or in a section thereof. This has all changed. Now, for instance, the decision by a Hollywood film-cartoon studio to grant a pay raise, with accompanying inroads on profit, can provide an additional stimulus to the continuing rise of cartoon making in Japan, where the costs of production are more than ten times less.

The decision to build a plant in France can have disastrous consequences if based on research findings valid for one European country only and if the widely differing mores and language barriers which exist throughout the continent have not been properly assessed. The decision by a large U.S. company to bring its massive resources and know-how to bear on promoting a new and economical substitute for coffee would have far-reaching reverberations in Brazil, Guatemala, and Colombia. In short, the potential damage which may be done by irresponsible or dishonest executives has become tremendous. No longer does the local entrepreneur in a small community simply live in the house on the hill and minister wisely or irresponsibly to the needs of the local people only. French housewives, Japanese children, Norwegian cheesemakers, Filipino professors,

Laotian farmers—all are influenced in some way by the decisions of U.S. executives.

The policy maker in the small, the medium, and the large company therefore has an implicit responsibility toward integrity which is often greater than that of most major politicians. In fact, the knowledge and character demonstrated by many management people qualify them to inject real doses of American free enterprise and integrity into the arteries of emerging nations. Already the European Common Market has begun to demonstrate what an alert and honorable alliance of businesspeople can accomplish.

Community Impact

Peter Drucker says:

> In an industrial society the only meaningful units of local government are enterprise and plant community. The decay of the traditional local governments, especially of town, city and county, is indeed primarily the result of the shift of focus to enterprise and plant community. Only in a society where enterprise and plant community are autonomous local self-governments, and where they carry and administer social security, will freedom be strong.[3]

Drucker has made a telling point here. With businesspeople declaiming long and loudly that government and politics have invaded many areas of the business community, the reaction has understandably produced negative results. Managers have often countered with facts labeled "Madison Avenue" and have sought to *justify* their position in the community rather than to *clarify* and *delineate* it. In other words, they have used superficial publicity devices to state how well meaning they are rather than build a solid awareness of their integrity by precept and example.

Consider, for instance, two rival companies in the same community. One has a true motivational climate, the other does not. No amount of hucksterish publicity on the part of the latter firm will bring the same net result in terms of wholesome community impact as the evident integrity of the other company.

* * *

In concluding this discussion of integrity in business, it should be said again that the job of the top executive is soul-wrenching and

[3] Peter F. Drucker, *The New Society,* Harper & Row, 1960, p. 338.

challenging as well as satisfying. He often becomes inexorably walled in by the complexities and protocol of modern business life. He often has few to whom he can turn for a close, personal evaluation and periodic reassurance. It has been demonstrated time and again, however, that the keystones of the productivity climate—above all, integrity—provide purpose and direction which are helpful indeed.

It is not utopian to push toward a type of business operation which could be labeled management by integrity. It is neither impossible nor impractical, but it does pose a real need for us all to explore new frontiers of tough-mindedness, human understanding, and effective communication.

In mapping out organizational strategy or formulating individual goals and objectives, all too few realize that the meaning of the words "strength" and "integrity" is the same. In other words, the integrity of a piece of material constitutes its strength and vice versa.

When we seek to discover and relate to the strength of others, we forge a relationship that has integrity.

Integrity is not just a "nice" word. It is the essence, the sum and substance, of all that is worthwhile.

19

Profile of a Tough-Minded Manager

A TOUGH-MINDED and motivational climate is impossible without tough-minded and productive individuals. And, while we must recognize that there are many variations, shadings, and types of people who can measure up to the tough-minded business requirements of tomorrow, we need a comprehensive set of common denominators. The specifications which follow may seem unrealistically ideal, but a sizable number of people have made the grade and have repeatedly demonstrated that stretching toward ideals which may initially seem impossible is really very desirable. It is necessary, in fact, to create "stretch" for the person who in turn intends to stretch his subordinates. People with flabby mental and physical equipment simply cannot meet the national and international requirements of business in the world of tomorrow.

As Individuals

Tough-minded managers must know themselves and be happy with what they are while at the same time building a healthy, calculated dissatisfaction with the status quo. They must realize, whether currently happy with their growth and caliber or not, that they must continue to grow, change, and stretch.

It is futile to point out that lots of nonmanagement people are more morose, disturbed, or neurotic than lots of management people. This has been tacitly implied throughout this book. But our concern in this particular context is management personnel, and we know it is naïve and silly to pretend that top executive status automatically implies optimum self-understanding, fitness, and effectiveness. People must take periodic, detailed inventories of themselves in terms of what they stand for, what they believe, what they can accomplish, what their strengths and weaknesses are, and what they put into life. The last-named point is perhaps most important. They must consider what they can give to life and derive from it rather than what *it* can give to *them*.

Here are some qualities of the ideal tough-minded executive as an individual, whether a man or a woman.

1. He practices self-discipline in terms of legal and ethical rules of conduct. He recognizes that a vigorous, outgoing, and sometimes ebullient way of life can only be possible and lasting as a product of such discipline.

2. He recognizes that developing and maintaining maximum physical fitness is an important requisite of mental health and acuity; that such fitness is not self-indulgence but part of an executive's obligation to his business, his employees, and his family. He becomes a bit of an authority on it and encourages his subordinates to do likewise. The development of the whole person is just lip service, he believes, without follow-through in terms of physical well-being.

3. He enjoys life—and people know it! The dour, scowling, formidable executive accomplishes little by his behavior except ulcers for his staff and himself.

4. His interests and activities may range widely or may center in certain worthwhile areas. At his best, the truly broad-gauge executive reads widely and has his own private development program.

5. He has either developed or is moving toward a personal faith. He feels that religion is a personal thing, a way of living, and is tolerant of the views of others. (Usually such beliefs and a zest for life are closely related.)

6. He never apologizes for a thing before doing it; he apolo-

gizes only when he knows he has not done his best. He is impatient with apologists because their contribution is always negative.

7. He takes the stand that negativism is *never* justified. He knows that there are pluses and minuses in many situations but that the minuses can become pluses. Minuses are really only the absence of pluses.

8. He always wants to know the *why* of a happening and supplies the *why* conscientiously to others.

9. He predicates his actions on facts but, knowing that the variables often exceed the constants, he is not hemmed in by them.

10. He is very much his own person and believes in God and himself.

11. He retains a healthy dissatisfaction with his abilities as a communicator. He knows eloquence is no substitute for understanding, erudition no guarantee of lucidity, volubleness no substitute for action. He does not confuse mere dialog with full communication.

12. He is impatient with old wives' sayings like, "You can't teach old dogs new tricks." He resolves to learn new things until the day he dies, and he knows he can. He retains his sense of wonder.

13. He slices right to the heart of problems and does something about them.

14. He knows that life without work is a short cut to deterioration.

15. He feels that a broad and eclectic fund of knowledge makes not only for a better generalist but also for a better specialist.

16. He is proud of his way of life and seeks to enrich the lives of others.

17. He does not confuse wit or intelligence with wisdom and strives steadily for greater wisdom.

18. He aims for a balanced existence in the full knowledge that wholesome recreation and rest habits enable him to do a better job.

19. He is impatient with the type of people who feel a harried expression and an ulcer are signs of success. He knows these people must grow up. He thinks laughter is great.

20. He is satisfied with nothing less than full success as a whole person.

21. He takes his work seriously but never himself.

As Members Society

A lot of bunkum has been written about the business executive's role in society. Points of view have been thrust forward which vary from pole to pole. Some say business should abdicate its rights to big government; others feel that business should virtually replace government in many areas (and this may be so); while still others talk vaguely about a kind of partnership heavily dominated by government.

It is the view of this book that government's role must change in expression and operation but not depart from basic principles. Our concepts of government must be fair and responsible as we move toward an increasingly cohesive world community, but this gradual transition must be accomplished in a statesmanlike way. Personalities and petty axes to grind will have no place tomorrow in either government or business. This calls for an enlightened and tough-minded citizenry of which business is a fully qualified representative.

Here are some specific things the tough-minded executive should do and is doing:

1. He lives integrity instead of relying on preachments.
2. He carries his emphasis on results over into his community and industrywide activities.
3. He practices candor widely and reflects a true warmth of feeling toward his associates.
4. He has the guts to say what ought to be said. He realizes the time for permissiveness and apologistic behavior by business men is long past (if it was ever appropriate).
5. He knows that the actions of a responsible executive are contagious and that there is virtually no limit to potential accomplishment if a sufficient number of people live the precepts of tough-mindedness.
6. He is a humanitarian, but no one ever labeled a tough-minded executive a "do-gooder."
7. He believes that management by integrity can be a rallying point for true social, political, and economic progress.
8. He believes in trying to strengthen the caliber of political and municipal officials rather than just commenting on it caustically.
9. He knows it takes more courage and ability to strengthen our society than it takes to highlight its weaknesses.
10. When broad problems loom, he is not content simply to ap-

point a committee. He wants target dates set, objectives defined—then action.

As a Manager

In his role within his own company, finally, the tough-minded person exemplifies all the principles of management by integrity as they have been set forth in these pages:

1. He takes steps to insure that the company's philosophy and objectives are researched, developed, and clearly communicated.
2. He insures that all employees know the *what, where, when, who, how,* and—above all—*why* of their jobs and the company.
3. He knows that people are more efficient and happy when they understand clearly what results are expected of them.
4. He insures that tailored procedures and techniques are installed to measure the contributions of all people and units to achieving the company's objectives, that compensation is related to performance.
5. He believes and lives the concept that the development of people, as a whole and in depth, pays real dividends to both the business and the individual.
6. He believes that everybody on the payroll should be held accountable for accomplishment, that he must do the job or get out of it.
7. He makes certain that the statement, "Management is the development of people, not the direction of things," moves briskly beyond the lip-service stage and becomes completely understood and operational.
8. He knows that all personnel will contribute and receive more if they are helped to develop a clear feeling of purpose, direction, dignity, and expectations.
9. He knows that optimum results cannot be expected unless each employee receives all information appropriate to the results required of him.
10. He strives to develop in all personnel an awareness of the value of work *to them.*
11. He believes in utilizing all the modern management tools fully when appropriate, but he insists that they pay their way.

12. He knows that management by integrity is realistic and workable; that, in reality, there is no fit substitute for it.

13. He knows that changes in business and the world in general are inevitable, but he doesn't resist them. He anticipates the unfolding of the future, plans for it, and sets trends.

14. He requires and encourages a climate conducive to innovation in all facets of the business.

15. He cultivates a curiosity for new dimensions of knowledge and resists efforts to predicate plans on past and present knowledge only.

16. He believes our country is on the verge of increasingly dramatic breakthroughs in both technology and human understanding and wants to play a positive role in them.

17. He does not look to others to charge his battery but takes the necessary action to build in perpetuating values, inspiration, and intellectual enrichment.

18. He realizes that pressures in the work environment and within the person are caused almost completely by negativism, pessimism, and ungrounded fears. Accordingly, he makes sure that his own beliefs, energy, and positiveness flow out steadily to the extremities of the business. This calls for tough-mindedness of the highest order and is a never-ending challenge.

19. He increasingly relegates tools and techniques to their proper secondary role as he moves toward mature conceptual management. For concepts are part of the stuff of wisdom, and wisdom is the stuff of management.

20. He is not deterred by small people. He knows what he wants and what the organization needs, secures maximum participation from his key people, and moves ahead relentlessly toward the actual practice of management by integrity.

The *summum bonum* of this tough-minded profile is herewith presented separately because it is at the heart of all the recommended elements in this book:

> *I will make the lives of others richer*
> *by the richness of my own.*

20

Our race for inner space.

The Challenge
of the Future

At the beginning of the decade we came to call the "soaring sixties," it seemed to many that we were entering a golden age. Certainly, the 1960s were eventful. We have seen the thrust of American free enterprise extended greatly all over the Western world. The 1970s have been, above all, a time of searching.

The standard of living has reached unparalleled heights for the majority of Americans. Jet travel, no longer at a glamorous premium, has become almost commonplace. Outer space continues to become more populated, even clogged, with space vehicles.

Let's pull together a few more of our achievements, and then let's look at them and attempt to see precisely where we are. We are a few million creatures on a piece of planetary material drifting—we hope, with purpose—through a vast and uncharted macrocosm. To what end?

Management practitioners, pundits, and ponderers have been greatly concerned with the following management basics for a number of years:

1. The management process.
      Plan.
      Organize.
      Execute.
      Coordinate.
      Control.
2. Involvement and commitment.
3. Management by objectives—call it what you will.
4. Results measurement.
5. Accountability.
6. Reduction of individual and intergroup conflict.
7. Communication and motivation.
8. Performance standards.
9. Organization planning and design.
10. Maximization of profit.

We've focused on these and they have paid off—at least partially I say "partially" because many individual supervisors and managers have encased themselves in an armor of restrictive and constrictive attitudes and values. We've shown our productive muscles to the world and proved we are the champs at producing abundance— abundance for the stomach and for the wallet. I'm not suggesting that we need apologize in any way for this. In point of fact, we must *accelerate* the development of managerial and technological innovations that are needed if we are to raise this level of abundance even higher.

The point, however, would remain obscure if we were to come to a permanent halt while we praise ourselves for this kind of achievement. The final goal—here and now, and perhaps forever—is to achieve abundance of the *human spirit*.

Let's take a look at a typical manager (call him Bert Farquhar) and determine how abundantly he is living.

Bert is 44; he is head of a major department in a medium-size company, which can be a bank, a store, or a manufacturing plant.

Bert pulls into the driveway of a house that costs somewhere between $35,000 and $65,000. Sometimes, as soon as he gets home, he reaches a little compulsively for a drink, but at other times he doesn't need one at all. He usually is glad to get home, although he often paces restlessly about the living room later in the evening. He doesn't know exactly why. He is vaguely uneasy and often becomes restless on Sunday because of a mixture of both dread and anticipation about going to work on Monday.

Bert is getting a little thick at the waist. He finds he is increasingly wearing out the heels of his shoes rather than the toes of them. He wonders from time to time whether his wife and family really love him or whether they just like the standard of living he provides.

He is beginning to take note of every newspaper article about men in their forties and fifties who have heart attacks. He's a little puffy-eyed: He wonders whether women still see him as a pretty virile and attractive guy. He has an obscure sense of yearning for a chance to prove it to a few of them.

He eats a good steak whenever he wants it. He buys good bourbon. He has two cars. His wife and children do not lack any material necessity; indeed, they have a number of luxuries.

Bert often has the feeling his subordinates are after his job and finds himself becoming more and more defensive and sarcastic with them. Tensions—although never serious ones—develop between him and his boss. He can seldom put his finger on the reason for these tensions. He has vague fears that he cannot identify. He has become quite uncertain of what success really is! He is hungry for something, but he doesn't know what. He is tired. He may drop dead in a few years or in a few months. He has a better bank balance than he dreamed of when he was a boy. He has a better car and a better home, and his children are going to better colleges.

Is Bert typical? Do you know him? Ever see him in the mirror? What's missing?

The answer is obvious: *abundance of spirit!* He has everything except the thing that most people yearn for most strongly—a feeling of significance, relevance, and value in this giddily spinning world. He is what Solzhenitsyn terms "spiritually exhausted."

Bert and his counterparts by the thousands and tens of thousands are fighting the battle of obsolescence as people and as managers. Sadly, most of them are not aware that their values, principles, skills, practices, and ideals are not sufficiently identified and integrated to form a viable system for living abundantly. Merely *existing* seems to be the goal. *Consuming* as a way of life has never met the test. Man must live for more than bread alone.

Tough-minded management—the mental toughness which suggests the qualities of leather rather than of granite—continues to be at a premium.

Dr. Edwin Henry, former manager of the Social Science Research Division of Standard Oil Company (New Jersey), has some interesting thoughts on this subject.

. . . The same kinds of people who are the effective managers today will be the effective managers in effective organizations in the year 2000.

I've been plagued over a period of years, in attempting to do studies on the identification of managerial potential, by the alibi that, well, it doesn't really do any good to study our organization now because 20 years from now we're going to require different kinds of people to manage this organization, and how do we know that the kinds that are successful today are going to be successful 20 years from now? The answer is, we don't know.

This is the same alibi that I heard 33 years ago. I submit that the people who started fresh out of college 33 years ago and became today's top management were bright people—but there are lots of ineffective, unsuccessful managers who are bright too. The successful men had high scholastic ratings in college, but so did many of the others. The successful men were ambitious, but the rest had ambitions too.

There *are* differences between the managers who have gotten to the top and the ones who didn't. These can be defined in terms of the creativeness, the innovativeness, and the tolerance for innovativeness in an organization. I've heard it said a great many times that the only man who can be an innovator in a particular organization is the boss—don't ever try to be one if you want to stay here, because the one thing he can't tolerate is creative people. But not only have effective managers got to tolerate change; they're the people who . . . started *planning* change, who *engineered* change, who were *change agents* in their organizations, who have made those organizations very different from what they once were.

I see no evidence whatsoever for assuming that these same kinds of people will not continue to innovate, plan, engineer, and become the agents for change in the next 33 years. As a stockholder, I hope that the corporations in which I own shares will elect the same kinds of people to manage them that have been managing for the past 33 years. In the year 2000 we're going to want organizations that have made the same kind of progress they have to date.[1]

Significant changes will certainly occur in the value systems of leaders—changes resulting in a greatly heightened interest in the positive potential of other people.

Here are some challenges for the person who wants to free him-

[1] Edwin Henry, in *Management 2000,* The American Foundation for Management Research (1968).

self from the straitjacket of obsolescence. These statements range from criticisms and recommendations to questions, all included for their sheer mental stretch and polemic worth.

1. Are you ready for the age of cybernetics, synergy, and synectics? (If you have to look up the meaning of two or more of these words, you may be pretty obsolete already.)
2. Did you know that the only usable equipment all of us take to work each day is our *minds?*
3. Would your subordinates continue to follow you if you had no rank, title, or vested authority? Would the quality of your *mind* expressed through *example* be sufficient?
4. Do you agree that the leading society in the world in the year 2000 will be the one that has won or is winning the race for *inner* space—the space between the ears?
5. Did you know that America produces approximately 50 percent of the world's wealth with 6 percent of the world's population? If we subtract all the nonbusiness people from that 6 percent we would have about 1 percent left. If we subtract all non-management people from that 1 percent we would have only a small fraction of 1 percent of the world's population represented by American business management. This fraction is the group that has been most responsible for the great increase in the world's level of material abundance.
6. What if this same group—these managers of American businesses—were to become informed, and committed to abundance of the human spirit? (Note the very last paragraph in this book.)
7. Foundations are allocating large sums for studies into the causes of violence and fear. Suppose greater amounts were spent to study the causes of compassion and confidence?
8. Suppose that business were to go all out to sponsor as well as carry out studies based on the following definitions of obsolete focus and modern focus? From studying symptoms to studying *causes?* For example:

Obsolete Focus	*Modern Focus*
Fear	Courage
Despair	Hope
Mental illness	Mental health
Sick businesses	Healthy businesses
Economic failure	Economic success

Obsolete Focus	*Modern Focus*
Dishonesty	Integrity
Fatigue	Energy
Dullness	Brightness
Cynicism	Positivism
Hate	Love
Insignificance	Significance
Faith	Doubt

There are, of course, many more, but do you see what we're calling for? *Mental toughness.* The person whose mental equipment is flabby will usually choose the easiest and most expedient course in his job, in his relations with his family, in his total existence.

9. Did you know that the most common denominator found by consultants in the organization that has failed, is failing, or is about to fail is finger-pointing, blame-fixing, reacting to symptoms rather than to causes—call it what you will? Whatever the label, it represents the dominance of a set of negative and expedient values.

10. The higher in the organization an executive moves, the greater the emphasis on qualitative abilities and results and the less the emphasis on quantitative abilities. By the time the executive becomes president his contribution is almost wholly in terms of qualitative individual skills (communication, motivation, and example), but he is measured by that implacable quantitative measurement we call the statement of profit and loss. Are most current management development programs built on this premise?

11. There is still a considerable gap between the lip service given to the importance of developing a sound, comprehensive philosophy of management, skillfully communicating it, and actually implementing such a philosophy.

12. How *practical* is a skillfully conceived and skillfully communicated management philosophy? One might just as well ask, "How practical is *motivation?*" To link these questions, it would be well to ponder the belief expressed by many psychiatrists that the principal cause of fatigue in America today is individual failure to have something bigger and more important than self to live for.

13. One of the most comfortable and expedient alternatives to tough-minded action for results is the temptation to couch

every word and deed in terms of what *they* will think. The tough-minded person knows the value of carefully assessing his contemplated action in terms of achieving the objectives that his own value system indicates are right and then moving vigorously to limit his self-commitment to the requirements of the situation.

14. We must recognize that *thought is the most productive form of labor*. This is easy to say, easy to parrot. However, management should be moving rapidly toward the active implementation of the policies, procedures, philosophy, processes, and practices based upon this premise.

15. We become what we think. Again, this is easy to say and easy to parrot, but the challenge implied here is enormous. Here are some relevant questions to ask and answer in order to implement the statement administratively.

    a. What do you know about what your employees really think? Traditional attitude surveys are not enough. It is suggested that laboratory methods (or sensitivity training), which are still in their infancy, hold real promise for use in house even at the hourly paid level.

    b. Do you yourself have a clear idea of what is needed to improve the value of the mind each subordinate brings to work each day? The *value* of your profit posture is usually squarely related to the *value* of your products, services, methods, and marketing skills.

    c. Have you ever studied the 20 greatest leaders in history with the full recognition that their actions were made possible only by the quality or value of their minds? A discussion of these values applied to current management problems is an eye-opener. It's astonishing to note how relevant they are now. Often the principal things lacking are the passion and guts to confront and apply them.

Two principal concepts represent within themselves a whole aggregate of tough-minded ancillary values. They are (1) management by example and (2) high expectations. Each of these depends for effectiveness and viability on the belief that we become what we think. Ralph Waldo Emerson said, in effect, that what you *are* speaks so loudly that nothing you say can be heard. In short, the example you provide is in a sense the sum total of you on display. Thus the overriding challenge becomes one of stoking the mind so that you are what you say and what you say is the product of the best program of individual development you can undertake. Only when we do this ourselves can we truly expect the best from subordinates and colleagues. *Attempting to change the behavior of others without changing our own is pretty nearly always futile.*

16. We do not defer to the dignity or worth of an individual when we expect little from him in terms of commitment, talent, and effort. We do not help him etch out his selfhood in a bland, permissive climate. He comes to know his strengths, his significance, his relevance when he is required to reach deep into his reservoir of strength, skill, and courage to confront the high expectations to which he has given his commitment.

17. If we find it comfortable and expedient to establish soft, comfortable, and expedient relations with our workers and colleagues, we are backing away from or oozing around the two concepts or systems of motivation which are really indivisible. Again, they are *management by example* and *high expectations* (of self first and of others second). You are warned, however, that it takes dedication, inspiration, and perspiration.

18. In common with everyone else, the tough-minded manager has two principal options as he moves along in life. These options may be expressed in several ways:

    a. Build or destroy. The manager can target and shape all of his ideals, values, and practices in terms of *building* or in terms of *destroying*. What rational person, you may ask, would focus on destruction? If he ignores the opportunity and challenge to use his mind and example to *build* people, products, profit, and so on, he has automatically—by abstention—elected to waste and destroy the potential for growth he possesses.

    b. Good or bad. He can assume either that people are fundamentally *bad* and must be coped with or that people are fundamentally *good* and his positive individuality can and will *build* a better department, a better company, or a better world.

    c. For or against. He can elect to express his abilities in terms of what he is *against* and become a futile, fragmented citizen, or he can elect to lead his family, build his enterprise, and function as a total citizen because he expresses his abilities in terms of what he is *for*.

19. *You can perceive and relate to the strengths of others only if you know your own.* In the absence of a clear and meaningful awareness of our strengths we are all too often likely to look for, perceive, and relate to the weaknesses of others. A focus on strength, not a preoccupation with weakness, is the only proven pattern for progress. Despair only begets despair. Hope and its concomitants, faith and love, can be nurtured only by hope, faith, and love. The dogged pursuit of despair will usually only result in further forging a black and vicious circle. A very wise and tough-minded leader said, "Love thy neighbor as thyself." In His wisdom, He knew that you must first possess something in order to be able to give it away. This tested commandment has a powerful contribution to make to the undergirding of managerial leadership and motivation.

20. Significant progress in the reduction of *conflict* within a unit (or a person) cannot be made until much greater effort is focused on how to discover and amplify the strengths of the individual. Our individual and collective guards fly up because of insufficient confidence, which stems from insufficient confrontation of strength-building problems. We must push for, call for, and exemplify a massive search for strengths throughout our society and shun the soft-minded expedient of crouching defensively behind what we are *against* and pointing out only the *weaknesses* of others. The tough-minded manager knows what he is *for* and knows such thrusts can be realized only by operating from a posture of strength.

The New Person

Throughout the world, we are hearing the rising challenge of young people. One columnist called them the "young insurrectionists." I don't know how accurate this description is, but I do know that many of them have beautiful ideals, and the older manager can often benefit greatly and experience fresh growth by *listening* to them and *thinking* about what they are saying. *The rebel knows what he or she is against and the individualist knows what he or she is for.* We have a generous mix of both types among the young.

The young are calling for the "new person" to appear on the scene and help bring about a better world. It is important to see that the new person the young are calling for to provide desperately needed economic, social, political, and spiritual leadership will not be found on some far-distant planet or in a laboratory or test tube.

Management at all levels must learn to see that this new person lies in the potential inherent in each of us. Casting aside the restrictive and constrictive wrappings of stereotypes concerning the true nature of management is imperative. That which has been safe and cozy to think about is no longer sufficient.

Recent newspaper headlines proclaim the rapidly increasing involvement of the businessperson in urban building and community improvement. We've already taken a strong step over the threshold *in this country,* but, with the escalating rate of international change and challenge, the tough-minded individual must be prepared to relate in a mentally tough way to the entire world around him.

Some Thoughts About the Future

The year 2000 is not many years away. We must do our level best to take off our economic, political, social, psychological, and spiritual blinders. Our methodology must accelerate in its shift from effect to cause, from treatment to prevention, from putting salve on the boil to purification of the bloodstream, from better military technology to better human minds—minds grounded in love, not hate, in building, not destroying.

Population

In the year 2000 there will be about 330 million people living in the United States. I believe approximately 80 per cent of the population of the United States is intellectually and morally obsolete with regard to the requirements of living a truly meaningful life even today. And this obsolescence cannot be allowed to remain or grow if we are to remove the nuclear sword of Damocles hanging over our heads.

If we truly accept a population explosion as a fact, we must also recognize that man's ability to "explode" into a pattern of action to solve birth-control problems is certainly not being demonstrated. Rather, we have retreated into a passive acceptance of what we conclude is inevitable and only shudder about the consequences. Money, energy, time, and thought must be targeted on *prevention*—not on after-the-fact *coping.*

The white population of the world is certainly inviting obsolescence when it fails to realize that it is vastly outnumbered by the black and yellow people. The solution? Accelerate our entire educational system to teach understanding, application, and ramification of the fact that *all* people must be judged by only one criterion: the *quality* of their moral commitment!

Labor

Increasingly we will see the dissolution of the typical labor-management contracts—contracts which reflect "legalese" and "loop-hole-itis" rather than the basic values and beliefs of individuals. Blue collar workers in the 1980s will have so much interaction with automated equipment on the job that the need for mental refreshment and challenge off the job (or as planned parts of the day's work) will be one of the challenges posed to both society as a whole and management educators in particular.

We will see much more emphasis on the building of an internal climate which is based on the belief that people—even a small group of them—who know what they are for are always in a better position to achieve uncommon objectives than two large factions that are fundamentally against each other. The potential for synergistic action and results is much greater.

The negative pattern has never yet proved its worth, but too few management and labor statesmen have been prepared to apply the necessary perspiration and *thought* in eliminating the *cause* of defensiveness, fears, and apprehensions. Continued roadblocks to understanding will exist until we recognize and accept the fact that our head, feet, and mouth are only instruments of the mind. Enlighten the *mind,* inspire it, direct it, and the symptoms (grievances, "gray sickness," arbitration cases, and so on) diminish in direct proportion. When both management and labor (aren't these terms obsolete?) experience abundance of spirit, the impact on the production of material abundance is amazingly positive.

One researcher says that by 1984 man will spend the first third of his life (25 years) getting an education, the second third working, and the final third enjoying the fruits of his labor. And here again we see evidence of obsolete projection, because if we truly believe that "by their fruits ye shall know them. . . ," we must see that we can come ever closer to a better understanding of who we are only by spending much of these 25 last years in giving to others the mental and spiritual fruits of the first 50 years. We will increasingly see that the go-giver gets most and the go-getter usually gets "got."

Education

Our educational mills continue to clank away and produce more and more "educated" people who possess M.A. and Ph.D. degrees. But we cannot fail to perceive a sterile and stale type of education emasculated by the exclusion of essential spiritual values. What about developing minds to *live,* rather than just *produce*? If the points of compatibility of the eight major religions of the world were taught, the "whole" student could perceive that the similarities vastly outnumber the differences. Think deeply about the ramifications of this. Perhaps herein lies the stuff of the new man which the insurgent younger generation is looking for the world over.

The distinguished psychoanalyst Erich Fromm states:

> Man today feels not impotent but lonely and anxious; he is also intensely bored. How could this be, many an incredulous or indignant reader will ask, when it is precisely one of the most valued traits of our culture that we are never bored? There is not a minute of unoccupied time. Boredom is related to the absence of inner aliveness, productive activity, genuine relatedness to the world, most fundamentally, perhaps, to the absence of love of life. Boredom is the opposite of joy, but modern man little knows what joy is. He knows what pleasure is, what fun is, what thrill is, but joy, that deep, glowing experience which requires no stimulus, which is serious and light at the same time, is a rare experience.

Does it not seem strange, almost eerie, that most of the studies of people and of the human condition have been and are still based upon research about and a preoccupation with illness? Medicine, psychology, psychiatry, sociology, even economics currently base most of their research on what has gone *wrong,* not what can go more *right.* Doesn't it seem strange that the young student of psychology is required to visit and observe only mentally ill people and to study their patterns of behavior at length? (And, of course, the medical student must spend much time with cadavers. On and on, ad infinitum, ad puzzlement.)

Psychologist Abraham Maslow is one shining exception to this. He has studied the "self-actualizer," the happy person. And his writings glow with realism based on hope, not despair—on light, not darkness. Psychologist Herbert Otto is also doing significant research that is focused on unleashing human potential.

What about targeted, massive educational efforts to study the causes of joy, health, achievement, not the causes of gloom, depression, sickness, and gold-bricking? It is urged and expected that education will have moved sharply in this direction by the year 2000. The equipment and techniques needed to implement teaching and learning can better be discussed by someone else. I am simply calling for a sprint toward the light, not a diffident retreat into the darkness. *We must confront our possibilities.*

Mental Abilities

People have traditionally exercised three major forms of power in relationship to other people. These are—

Legal power.
Economic power.
Mental power—the authority of the mind—by example.

History is replete with examples of leaders whose political or legal power was anything but permanent. Adolf Hitler had both legal and economic power but suffered a degrading and infamous death. He left behind no legacy of love, respect, truth, hope, or light. His relatively short reign, terrible in its mental illness, will be only a faint and pathetic low-water mark in the tide of history.

In unleashing the potent but still relatively dormant minds of people, real and urgent priority should be given to wrenching our minds away from agonizing over our frailties and inadequacies toward developing better awareness and understanding of our strengths. Sober reflection suggests that we may face seemingly insurmountable difficulties here unless we are able to do something fundamentally different in the education of teachers—particularly those who work at the university level.

It must cease to be "intellectually" fashionable to engage only in dissent and debunking. A cynical assault on the fundamental truths of the Bible will yield nothing but fragmented cynicism. For instance, you cannot break the Ten Commandments, you can only break yourself. Its eternal truths *are*. Rather, the real task of the intellectual can, should, and probably will be the discovery of better methods and techniques of understanding and applying these truths. Suppose that the average executive made a strong attempt to understand and apply Immanuel Kant's *Critique of Pure Reason* to his daily job. This would require real pragmatic intellectuality and could produce a kind of mental toughness which would in turn contribute much to both personal and company objectives.

Economic empires can be created and become ever greater or they can vanish virtually overnight. The secret of retaining economic power lies squarely in the demonstrated ability to apply one's mind in a wise and positive way in the use of wealth resources. In short, the perpetuation of meaningful and viable *economic* power is utterly dependent on mental power.

In the last analysis, then, the question should be asked: Is legal and economic power anything more than a transient myth without mental power? I think not.

Our mental potentials will begin to be more rapidly realized when we begin to shed the accumulated stereotypes of the past and begin to act on the assumption that all people are fundamentally good if permitted to be so. Frank Nunlist, former chairman of the board of the Worthington Corporation, has spoken convincingly on this subject.

> Two-thirds of the 20th century has passed. Immediately ahead lies the last third of the last century of the second millennium since Christ. We live in a world of violence and turmoil. Wars, thankfully relatively small ones, break out around the world. There are threats and outbreaks in the Congo, in the Middle East, in Vietnam, on the Chinese-Indian border, in Hong Kong. Crime and violence run rampant on our streets at home. College campuses around the world are in revolt.
>
> This is indeed a time to take stock of our world and its society and to determine, if we can, what approaches, what attitudes, and what means a new leadership must take if we are to move people toward the goals for which they were truly destined. This last third of this century may mark a turning point in the affairs of man. I believe, in fact, that it will—providing men of goodwill determine that this be so. I believe that we stand on the threshold of a new renaissance in the affairs of man. I believe that we are about to exchange will for idea in the world. I believe that the fulcrum will shift from power to persuasion, from physical force to creative intelligence.
>
> It is a time to find out why our leadership has failed to produce better understanding, better results both domestically and internationally, and more rapid progress toward man's God-given right to

life, liberty, and the pursuit of happiness. . . . As much as we like to engage in crystal-ball gazing, in the art of prophecy, I cannot but feel that changes in our society and its leadership will develop only as our society is prepared to accept change. . . .

The year 2000 seems a long way ahead to you and to me. Yet it is only 33 years from now. The young man who graduates from college this year will, in the year 2000, be about my own present age. This young man's challenge, his need for knowledge, his ability to achieve personal satisfaction will be far greater and far more complex than we can now visualize. And this young man 33 years hence is going to have to lead an entirely different following from what we know today. He will need to be a leader among men whose needs to satisfy their hunger and keep themselves and their families clothed and sheltered will no longer predominate. He will lead men whose desires move in a variety of directions. The needs of the young and the needs of those who have retired are quite different from the needs of those who work. In his first 30 years the manager of the future will be maturing through a variety of processes. For his second 30 years he will be leading the improvement in standards of living, after which he will emerge into a world of security for himself with a desire to help others become equally secure.

From these inevitable changes in man's expenditure of his time and energy will come, I believe, a greater desire for individualism as people flee from the protective mantle of mass production, mass marketing, and mass identification. I suggest to you, therefore, that George Orwell may not have been accurate when he projected a leadership by Big Brother for a faceless society. I believe that the characteristics of our society will be far more varied than they are today and that Big Brother and Big Father will not be wanted or accepted.

What will be wanted will be thoughtful, creative, imaginative, understanding, intelligent leadership—leadership that will be effective because its reasoning toward the common weal is valid, sound, and thoughtfully conceived; leadership that shuns the use of power, manipulation, and fear. There is no doubt in my mind that leadership by thought will replace leadership gained through the power of money, the power of politics, the power of military might, or the power of personality. . . .

The leader of the year 2000 will be a very young man. His goals will be broad and his influence great. He will reason from the particular to the general and will look outward at the conflict of forces to see that they are kept in balance and in proper perspective. He will realize the great strengths that lie in the point and counterpoint of individualism. He will spend more time in creating satisfactions for people as individuals and will tend to destroy some of our present concepts of mass management. He will understand that man is neither a machine nor a physical animal, but is endowed with creative intelligence, creative drive, and the will for good, not merely the insensate will to live.[2]

Longer Life

Erich Fromm says that as a nation our "passion for consumption" expresses our effort to find "an escape from and a compensation for anxiety." And in this search, he says, man is "eternally expectant—eternally disappointed."

Studies of centenarians and people in their eighties and nineties reveal that most of them were not "consumers" but doers and builders. Dr. Frederick J. Stare, chairman of the nutrition department of Harvard University's School of Public Health, had this to say when asked whether stress and strain bring on heart trouble.

> As far as I know there is no evidence that stress and strain have anything to do with causing heart disease. This is about the opposite of what most people think.
>
> I think most people are going to be happier and have much better health if they work hard physically and mentally.

Dr. Stare might agree that an important proviso could be inserted here. Hard work focused on the *building* and *development* of something positive will usually aid in developing and maintaining positive health. Hard work focused on *tearing down* or focusing on what one is *against* can have deleterious effects on health.

As the year 2000 draws nearer, I believe we can, accordingly, do much to lengthen life through changed attitudes (exclusive of the marvelous breakthroughs beginning to take place in medicine and biochemistry). It has been heartening indeed to note the continuous acceleration of the study and application of mental toughness by an increasing number of restless and energetic managers both here and abroad.

Genetic Engineering

Predictions here must be left to the geneticists themselves. We can only hope that the goals toward which this science is moving are

[2] Frank J. Nunlist, in *Management 2000*, op. cit.

in consonance with the value system in this book. That science itself might become an idol rather than a tool for releasing man's *ultimate potential for good* is an unlikely possibility.

Medicine

I anticipate that medicine will increasingly direct its efforts to the study of wholeness, health, and *preventive* maintenance. Highly organized and controlled studies of what produces health and longevity rather than disease and death are expected. The transplantation of human hearts is a thrilling breakthrough, but the ability to rebuild and replace diseased heart tissue through diet, drugs, or other methods would be infinitely more thrilling. We have studied communities with an unusually high incidence of cancer, but we must focus more of our efforts on studying communities where cancer is virtually *nonexistent.*

Nuclear Energy

The awesome potential of controlled nuclear energy etches out the necessity of deciding whether we believe man is fundamentally good or fundamentally bad. This basic decision will undergird the whole structure which follows. Hence, either we will concentrate on building weapons with a maniacal intensity or we will make massive efforts to use peaceful nuclear instruments to amplify our productive and harmonious potential.

John Dewey said, "Change in the climate of the imagination is the precursor of the changes that affect more than the details of life. . . ." The bomb which shattered Hiroshima was developed in a climate of war—that is to say, in a climate of hate and fear. We can arrive at the most effective uses of nuclear energy well before the year 2000 only in a climate that is aerated by spiritual values.

New Worlds to Conquer?

Let's lift our sights. It's a small world, we say. But for how long? Space travel is no longer a subject purely for the fantasy world of children who read comic books and adults whose favorite light reading is science fiction. In the words of *The Rensselaer Review,* "Many qualified scientists feel that it will be possible to colonize the planets for farming, mining, and military purposes by the year 2025. Planets as military bases are very real possibilities." Nor is this an isolated opinion. *Advertising Age* quotes E. B. Weiss:

> . . . great astronomers (Dr. Harlow Shapley of Harvard is one) are convinced that superior intelligence exists "out there"—and when we establish communications with those superior minds, the present knowledge explosion will become just a tiny "pop." Can you imagine having a million years of advanced extraterrestrial knowledge suddenly made available to homo sapiens?[3]

Will our planet one day participate in intergalactic and extraterrestrial relationships? And, if so, will we approach these new worlds with an attitude that we are superior beings who have set out to colonize, establish military bases, and run things in our own way? We don't know. Perhaps we will never know. But while we wait and ponder, we might do well to shift our sights from a dogmatic conquest of outer space to an enlightened conquest of inner space.

Some New Tools

It was stated earlier that the person who needed to look up the meaning of words like synergy, cybernetics, and synectics might be pretty obsolete already. Let's add the phrase, "actualization of human potential" to this list and attempt to show diagrammatically the relationship of these terms to laboratory or sensitivity training. This is considered important because the potentiality of this system of techniques is enormous. The "new" man or woman needs new methods of self-discovery—or, perhaps, only a skilled modern sophistication about known truths in a relevant context.

Human progress is slow, sometimes unsteady, but constant. Human possibilities are virtually unlimited if the motive thrust of people is fueled by a viable, positive, and relevant system of values. The challenge to the tough-minded person is great and can lead to a series of thrilling and zestful confrontations. But the hazards are also great, especially if we confuse the search for self-actualization and its emphasis on strengths with the search for self-destruction with its emphasis on weaknesses.

Exhibit 1 illustrates the ascent from a preoccupation with the requirements of the stomach and wallet to an impatient quest for

[3] E. B. Weiss, *Advertising Age* (December 11, 1967).

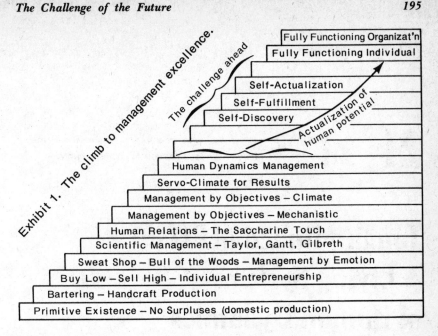

Exhibit 1. The climb to management excellence.

greater significance as a fully functioning person. It shows the evolution of management from static, stratified structures to a synergistic process. The result will be a fluid, dynamic, and very responsive *whole* made up of fluid, dynamic *individuals* who possess strong feelings of purpose, relevance, and *significance*. The search for full functioning of the self promises, through much human behavioral research, to be the most fruitful endeavor the modern and relevant manager of organizational enterprise can undertake. The potential yield from the sophistication of the tools of money, material, time, and space will continue to be limited until new breakthroughs are made in the understanding of *people*. A brand new look at the nature of objectives is an important early step. Objectives will need to be formulated and stated in terms of *qualitative* objectives with more sophisticated use of *quantitative measurement*.

 In summary, remember that the tough-minded person—the tough-minded manager—will increasingly pursue a life of *tough* rational purpose, and, above all, a surging awareness of the *joy of building*.

21   *The central purpose of managing by objectives is to make effective use of the strengths of the organization to achieve objectives.*

Tough-Minded MBO— A Living System of Human Dynamics

I⊤ is axiomatic to say that management is the development of people and the full and effective utilization of them to achieve objectives. It is not so commonly recognized, however, that the total composition of the workforce is the sum of people's individual and collective *strengths*.

The *mechanisms* of MBO with which we are all familiar are essential—in fact, crucial. But these structures, these aggregates of procedures, can never become living management systems unless and until we identify, classify, assign, expect, measure and control the strengths of the *people* who make up the system.

Consider with me some of the key "qualitative" elements in such a system. They include:

Human significance
Human growth
Human possibilities

The Need for Significance

I am emphasizing human significance here because it is primary and essential to all human growth and to the actualization of all human possibilities.

Humans are delightful skinsful of variables. They are unpredictable, changeable, mercurial, often frustrating—but *always* challenging, unique, and important. How can we get to know people quickly and well? One important way is to seek diligently to discover their strengths, because each person is the *sum of these strengths*. Weaknesses are only missing strengths; they only confuse us and indicate what the other person is *not*. How can we help people to feel significant and worthwhile? One of the best ways is to constantly *look* for and *expect* their best. In this way we begin to employ the "principle of high expectations." *Second*-rate expectations suggest second-rate regard for others. First-rate expectations say clearly and distinctly, "I think you're first-rate. I esteem and value you."

How do we build warm, spontaneous, delightful relationships with others? We do all we can to insure that the person we see in the mirror *is* and *feels* warm, spontaneous, and delighted with the opportunities and challenges implicit in each day.

Human relationships add *life* to life. Loneliness, or the lack of human relationships, *deadens* and stills the throbbing possibilities of day-to-day living. There are so many, many opportunities to strengthen, enrich, and vitalize lives through tough-minded caring, sharing, and daring.

We all have needs. They, of course, vary in degree, intensity, and method of fulfillment. They define, perhaps more than anything else, what we call individual differences.

Most everyone is familiar with Abraham Maslow's hierarchy of needs and with Frederick Herzberg's concept of needs. I believe there is one need which undergirds, suffuses, and transcends all others. It is, I believe, the most important need of all and is indivisibly related to responsible performance.

This central and compelling need is one of a feeling of *significance*. The virtual compulsion to fulfill this need lies at the root of negative, troublesome, and even bizarre behavior. It also lies at the root of joyful, productive, and developmental behavior.

For instance, the accident-prone person is saying by his actions: "*Notice* me, I need to feel significant." The rapist, dictator, or murderer is saying: "*React* to me, I need to feel significant as a human being."

At the opposite end of the scale, the person who is well along on the path of wholesome self-discovery, self-fulfillment, and self-actualization usually feels no need for the violent, the negative, the bizarre. He or she is *becoming* and knows this through a sense of *achievement* and other related indices. Such a person's significance grows with the discovery of his or her capabilities in response to expectations. I feel it is a responsibility in this context to point out two key omissions in Dr. Maslow's hierarchy of needs. They are faith and hope.

"Becoming" in Response to Expectations

I submit that one of the best ways to encourage present social- and work-related disintegration is to continue to encourage permissiveness—provide rewards not related to responsible performance and behavior and just plain "keeping our brother" in a host of ways. I use this phrase only to refer to those situations in which one's "brother" could actually be taught to *keep expectations*.

The central premise of this message is that we can best help a person to discover himself, etch out his uniqueness and individuality, and grow in confidence and significance when we care enough (in the real tough-minded and tenderhearted sense) to:

Constantly look for the person's best.
Consistently *expect* that best.
Insure that compensation is related directly to performance.
Relate all of the foregoing to the organizational objectives of the employer.

It is much easier to look for and expect a person's second best or worst, and thus enhance his or her feelings of *in*significance if we are in the habit of expecting those same, easy, second-rate things from ourselves. Without thoughtfully conceived and mind-stretching objectives, it is difficult, indeed virtually impossible, to *express* such expectations effectively.

In a macrocosmic sense, I even submit that wars are declared and other terrible mass happenings occur because someone or several people felt terribly inadequate and insignificant.

In the on-the-job sense, I submit that all the usual "undesirable" indices, such as turnover, absenteeism, and low morale, would be vastly reduced if all employees felt more significant and useful.

The defense mechanism of "compensation" or "overcompensation" is well known, and I believe most major and minor destructive acts in our culture would have been avoided if people felt sufficiently significant. Again, we can only experience growing measures of this feeling when we know we are "using" ourselves well, when we are moving toward meeting our own positive expectations or those of others, when we are carrying out with conviction the commitments in which we have been effectively involved.

It is important to understand the difference between self-esteem and significance. For instance, one might feel a good and reasonable measure of self-esteem, but still feel underchallenged, underutilized, and underactualized, and therefore less than fully significant. A high measure of significance means that we see the person in the mirror as more than someone we *accept*. Rather, we feel *right* about ourselves. The Bible tells us: "The Kingdom of God is within you," "You are the light of the world," "You are the salt of the earth," and gives many other similar assurances. Of course, we need love and respect from others, but we won't feel fully *significant* about ourselves unless our "conscience" tells us we are employing, using, and constructively *realizing* our possibilities. High expectations, expressed in sound, mind-stretching objectives, speak to those deep needs and help us fuse and focus our human resources. Here are some crucial ancillary elements of significance:

- We feel significant when our work helps provide us with purpose and *direction*—hence, *objectives*.
- We make further gains as we reach out to the world around us with a sense of wonder, growth, and stretch—again, our key aid is *objectives*.
- We take significant steps to deal with our wants, needs, and problems when we can articulate our *objectives*.

The Human Element and MBO

Now let us examine the seven phases that constitute the human system which undergirds, stretches, and nourishes the mechanisms of the effective MBO system.

Exhibit 2 presents a "circle of strengths" that illustrates what should be happening concurrently with the more typical systematic processes shown in Exhibits 3 and 4 on pages 202–204. Within the framework of these seven phases, I am illustrating just a few of

Exhibit 2. A servo system of strengths management.

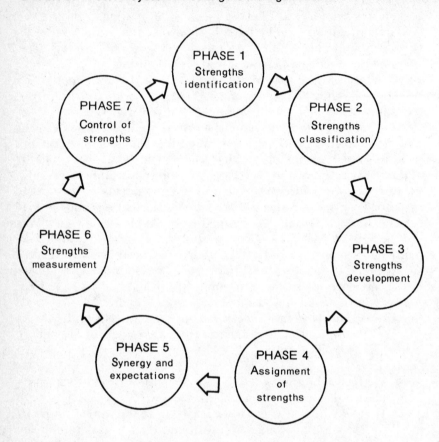

the key elements required for active operation. The discussion can serve as a basis for beginning a strengths-management system in your organization.

Phase 1. Strengths Identification

Determine the reality of the individuals—their strengths—and thus determine the real capacity and potential of the organization.

- Complete individual inventories by all members of management. Search for real and demonstrated as well as hoped-for strengths.
- List "victories" (past experiences). These are happenings

wherein the manager achieved a measure of what he or she hoped for.
- List individual objectives and relate them to job (company, divisional, departmental) objectives. These should indicate strengths which can contribute directly to job results.

All too often, it is assumed that employees *know* their personal objectives. In reality few do. In this living MBO system, it is recommended that updated, improved versions of the individual counseling approach used in the Hawthorne studies at Western Electric be researched for use. It is my belief that the bottom line—the most unerring indication of strengths deployment—will be greatly improved by making an organizational investment in helping all employees really begin to think through and work out personal objectives for themselves.

- Look for elements of unique strengths found in products, services, and so on. Include those which can contribute directly to "bottom-line" indices.
- Conduct interviews and *listen* for strengths. Don't get bogged down and preoccupied with weaknesses.

To continue to conceive of MBO as an aggregate of static mechanisms, and not as a living aggregate of strengths, is a velvet trap. Large doses of courage, initiative, and innovativeness are needed.

Phase 2. Strengths Classification

Determine precisely what the relative kinds and types of strengths are. Know what you can extract, expect, and utilize from your "bank of organizational strengths."

- Prepare anecdotal records listing key strengths of your team members. A primary step here is to ask the group to provide you with a thought-out list of their strengths classified according to their priorities.
- Categorize the inventories for practical and applied use. Look for:

    Decision-making strengths—evaluation skills.
    Problem-solving strengths—analytical skills.
    Face-to-face strengths—communication skills.

Exhibit 3. The cyber-climate for results (organization development).

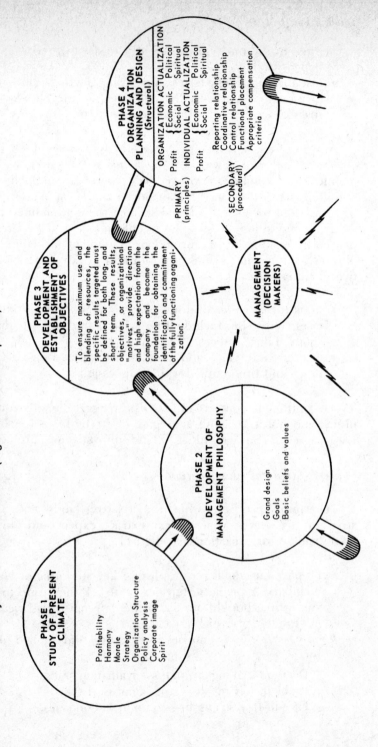

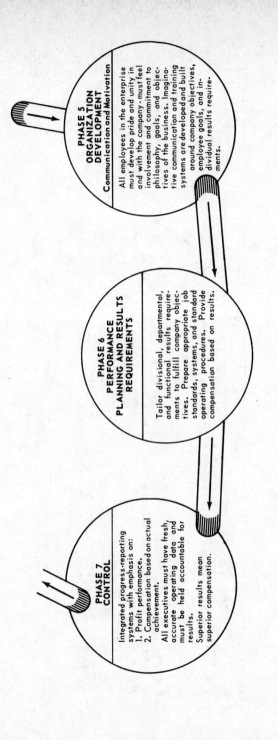

**PHASE 5
ORGANIZATION
DEVELOPMENT**
Communication and Motivation

All employees in the enterprise must develop pride and unity in and with the company - must feel involvement and commitment to philosophy, goals, and objectives of the business. Imaginative communication and training systems are developed and built around company objectives, employee goals, and individual results requirements.

**PHASE 6
PERFORMANCE
PLANNING AND RESULTS
REQUIREMENTS**

Tailor divisional, departmental, and functional results requirements to fulfill company objectives. Prepare appropriate job standards, systems, and standard operating procedures. Provide compensation based on results.

**PHASE 7
CONTROL**

Integrated progress-reporting systems with emphasis on:
1. Profit performance.
2. Compensation based on actual achievement.
All executives must have fresh, accurate operating data and must be held accountable for results.
Superior results mean superior compensation.

Exhibit 4. Organizational development: a total system for managing by objectives.

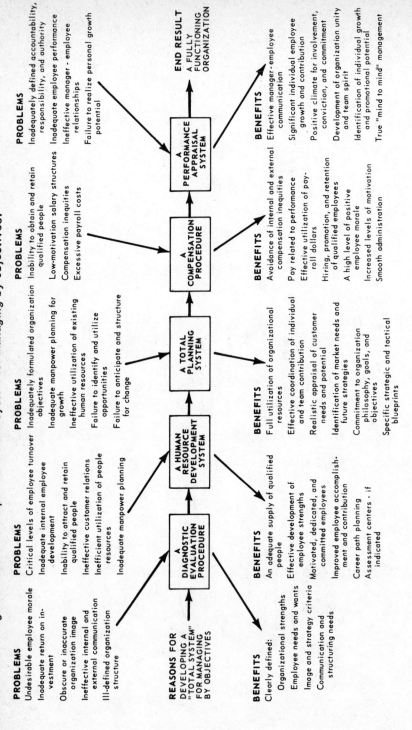

- List degrees of strength—from major to minor. It is important to know weaknesses so that you can determine just what additional strengths are *needed* or what is needed to develop *existing* strengths further.

Phase 3. Strengths Development

Policies, procedures, and practices are designed to increase the strengths and the effectiveness of all personnel, in terms of performance.

- Preparation and dissemination of a companywide philosophy stressing strengths development.
- Research to determine training and development needs and specific requirements.
- Preparation of a thoughtful strengths-development plan.
- Implementation of the plan—for example:
  Specifically designed modules
  Assessment centers
  Career path planning
  Carefully designed assignment of position and job content
  Provision of specific strengths-actualization information
  Personnel planning
  Other elements

You cannot "develop" mechanistic elements such as equipment, paper, floorspace, and written processes. You can develop only living human strengths.

Phase 4. Assignment of Strengths

The implications here for high individual and organizational morale are enormous. Essentially, the proper and full use of one's strengths is the greatest single need of people.

- Demonstrated and tested strengths—in actuality, this is what people are paid for. It is *performance!* Use these strengths where they will be the most effective in helping both the individual and the company meet their goals.
- Suspected strengths—these can be verified and rewarded only by *stretching* assignments.
- Expected strengths—help employees discover *who* they are,

what they can be and what they can *do;* this is one practical way to describe and understand the process of "leadership."

Be prepared to depart from basing assignments on mechanistic assumptions of the "traditional roles" of women, men, minorities, and other groups. Shift from ROLE orientation to GOAL orientation, thus bringing strengths fully to bear.

Phase 5. Synergy and Expectations

- Expectation instruments—tools for the ongoing management job.

  Positive accountability provisions—accountability, properly conceived, is always to focus and maximize the use of strengths and never to become preoccupied with weaknesses.

  Results expected—statements of what you want *done.* Such commitments should be products of sound discussion and involvement sessions.

  Performance standards. These will help determine how *well* the job should be done.

- Training and counseling of your human resources. Some key requirements are:

  Positive listening—really *hear* their wants, needs, and problems.

  Vulnerability and openness—we grow and discover new capacities and abilities only by being vulnerable and open in interacting with the requirements of life and work.

  Flexibility and versatility—rigidity is like rigor mortis. Life and growth are synonymous with supple attitudes and practices.

- The "principle of high expectations"—this is central to a living system of MBO.

  Express caring. Keep trying to evoke the best in others. To do less is to indicate *lack* of caring.

  Motivate. Help clarify the individual motives (objectives) of the manager and relate them to the motives (objectives) of the organization.

  Clarify. Surface and require use of each individual's strengths.

Stretch. Require the individual to reach deeply within to find the strengths to increase quality or quantity of performance.

Build teamwork and real self-esteem. We can truly respect ourselves and reach out cooperatively to others only when we feel we have done, and are doing, reasonably tough or difficult things.

Although the end results of such synergy are "objective" measurements (for example, money), the capacity to generate the optimum measure of these results stems directly from, and in proportion to, the use of "subjective" strengths like *thought, emotions,* and *attitudes.*

Phase 6. Strengths Measurement

Measure the strengths of people, money, materials, time, and space by overhauling all policies, procedures, processes, practices, and programs to reflect strengths emphasis, which should be incorporated into the following:

Annual reports. Describe new possibilities inherent in the resources (people, money, materials, time, and space) of the organization.

Budgets and forecasts. Include "possibility" thinking which moves beyond the typical comparisons with past achievements.

Profit plans—Organization manuals. See budgets and forecasts.

Policy manuals. Insure that all standard operating policies and procedures are redesigned and rewritten to reflect strengths emphasis.

Progress reports. Stress progress toward objectives rather than weaknesses or deviations.

Strength audits. Systematically measure actual performance compared to estimated possibilities.

Manpower inventories. Reflect present and projected estimates of strengths resources. (In reality, the *only* resources of an organization are its strengths.)

Visual inspection.

Memoranda.

Committees. They must insure that all discussions, plans, and actions make the shift from "trouble-shooting" to "possibility shooting."

Phase 7. Control of Strengths

- Positive listening. The terms "positive" and "strength" are synonymous, just as "negative" and "weakness" are synonymous. We can listen positively only if we feel secure in our awareness of our own strength. As a manager, you can respect others only if you respect yourself. You can care about others only if you can care about yourself. You can lead others only if you can lead and direct yourself. In sum, you can relate to and *listen* to others only if you can understand yourself and feel good about that self.
- Compensation related directly to *demonstrated* strengths—results.
- Performance appraisal—managerial assessments, incident files, and face-to-face interaction that build on strengths rather than focusing on weaknesses.

These are only thought-provokers. The way from mechanistic notions of MBO to a living system of MBO will be fraught with challenges and difficulties because of the weakness orientation and conditioning of our contemporary society. As organizations begin to truly sense the "possibilities" in an all-out emphasis on strengths, however, we will increasingly see static and mechanistic "programs of MBO" growing into organismic "living systems"—the kinds of systems that evoke, unify, and blend the most precious and practical resources of people into a viable, self-perpetuating, and self-renewing organic whole. The potential is so enormous that we must not delay.

22

MBO is the central gearbox of organizational actualization.

The Fully Functioning Organization

OD or OA?

The proliferation of nostrums, gimmicks, recipes, and panaceas dealing with a sound, pragmatic thing like organization development can be viewed as dismaying, amusing, or appalling. Resolutely reduced to the abbreviation OD, it has virtually become a fad wherein many younger students of management literally believe that a mishmash of programs, courses, experiments, and games are what it's really all about. Let's attempt some clarity, priorities, and logic:

1. Does management expect the bottom line to reflect *development* or the actualized *product* of development?
2. Does management want to pay for the development and continuous introduction of new *programs* or an effective payload delivery *system?*
3. Does management want supervisors and managers at all levels to engage in increased *activity* or *results?*

It may be obvious that I am saying that the fully functioning organization is one in which all resources of the organization are logistically blended to *actualize* its objectives.

Many top executives indicate piously that "we are doing our best to manage by objectives, but things haven't really changed that much. I don't see what the big deal is about MBO."

If a "program of MBO" is to become truly the kind of total system for managing by objectives from top to bottom and side to side in the organization, it must go far beyond the mere *setting* of objectives. When objectives have been well developed as a product of effective research, involvement, analysis, and evaluation, when they have been thoughtfully and thoroughly communicated, when commitments and control dates are in place, MBO is *not* under way. Only the objectives themselves have been established. Real *management* is what happens from then on.

The kind of total *system* of MBO which comprises the central organ of OD or, better yet, OA (organization actualization) requires that the philosophy, policies, procedures, processes, programs, and personnel are all conditioned to relate all decisions and activities regarding the objectives. As this begins to happen, the organization begins to *actualize* its capacity to achieve objectives.

All too often in the company that is purporting to "practice MBO," the compensation policies and procedures are still geared to rewards based on seniority, academic credentials, personal qualities, volume of activities, old school ties, ad nauseam. This is *not* management by objectives!

Let us examine the implications of what we've just described as a fully functioning organization:

Philosophy should be carefully thought through, discussed thoroughly, and then communicated at all levels of the organization. It should be made clear that performance appraisals, compensation, and all other decisions *will* and *must* be keyed directly to performance.

Policies will reflect the above and will also be keyed to the strengths concepts discussed in the preceding chapter. Studs Terkel in *Working* says: "Most jobs are bigger than most people."[1] Tough-minded policies will stretch people's minds and require them to grow into jobs that grow in consonance with living and changing objectives.

---

[1] Studs Terkel, *Working: People Talk About What They Do All Day and How They Feel About What They Do* New York, Pantheon Books (1974).

Procedures are specifics which illustrate, for instance, how the point system of job evaluation can still be relevant and desirable in the actualized organization if its *factors* are changed to reflect indices of performance, rather than activity.

Processes are procedural components that are implemented daily, so that it is evident that all decisions must be keyed to (*a*) building on strengths and (*b*) making objectives happen.

Programs should all be conceived within the following context: "What will its contribution to objectives be?"

Personnel is where it all must come together. People usually perform best in the organization that has accomplished the following transition:

From	*To*
Role orientation	Goal orientation
"Importance"	Significance
Insecurity	Significance
Programs	System
Vague, adequate expectations	Clear, stretching expectations
Defensiveness	Open, warm, thoughtful candor
Activity documents and reports	Progress documents and reports
Hunch and guess	Disciplined decisions
Inconsistency	Consistency
Conformance	Individuality
Competing with others	Competing with self
Complexity	Simplicity
Avoidance of problems and needs	Confrontation of problems and needs
Dialog	Communication
Crises and fire-fighting	"Early-warning systems"
Office politics	Team synergy
Blurred, expedient morality	Tough, stretching moral climate
Reaction related to symptoms	Action related to causes
Disparate, dissonant actions	Unity
Compensation based on actions and personal characteristics	Compensation based on positive performance
Fragmentation	Purpose and direction
Getting	Giving
Preoccupation with weaknesses	Building on strengths
Commitment to self only	Commitment to goals and objectives which transcend self
Benign neglect	Caring
Negative listening	Positive listening
Dissatisfaction (past-oriented)	Unsatisfaction (future-oriented)

From	*To*
"Gamesmanship"	Accountability for results
Superficial preoccupation with be-havioral science jargon and patois	Analysis, evaluation, synthesis, and synergy of tough-minded pos-sibilities
"Affirmative-Action" jargon and "dialog"	Evaluating *all* people on the basis of performance

Considerations for the Future

Minorities

"Minority" groups are generally thought to include women, blacks, and youth. The tough-minded manager believes it is coun-terproductive to engage in strident complaints about the injustices of the past. He or she admits they were sick and deplorable and feels compassion for the victims. But such a person rigorously refuses to become bogged down in an enervating and vitiating focus on the *past!*

He or she believes that life and work will become immensely more exciting and worthwhile in direct proportion to the goal of full equality. The tough-minded manager believes that confident and emotionally secure men respect and accept strong, actualized women (and all other "minorities") as colleagues, partners, and friends. This type of manager insists that precisely the same yardstick for recogni-tion and reward be used for all these minorities. That yardstick is *performance.*

Furthermore, the tough-minded manager is committed to *helping* such equality and justice *happen.* He or she will *expect,* not insist; will *lead,* not just complain.

The Will to Manage

For those who have, or are developing, the *will* to lead and man-age, I offer the following thoughts of Mortimer J. Adler:

> We often think of ourselves as living in a world which no longer has any unexplored frontiers. We speak of pioneering as something of the past. But in doing so, we forget that the greatest adventure of all still challenges us—what Mr. Justice Holmes called "the adven-ture of the human mind." Men may be hemmed in geographically, but every generation stands on the frontiers of the mind. In the

world of ideas, there is always pioneering to be done by anyone
who will use the equipment with which he is endowed. The great
ideas belong to everyone.

Need I say more?

Although I have meant every word in all the preceding pages, I
want to close on a light and buoyant level. Please join me in the following vicarious "adventure."

The Peter What?

or

Protean Placebo

The whimsical and titillating book entitled *The Peter Principle*[2] is
really delightful reading, particularly—and here is my thesis—for
the obsolete or near-obsolete person who wants a reassuring pallia-
tive for the expedient batch of obsolete practices for which he or she
has opted.

The "principle" reads like this:

> *In a hierarchy every employee tends
> to rise to his level of incompetence.*

Ah! What a delicious challenge in an age and on a planet wherein we
still know relatively nothing about full human potential. I can picture the young college or high school student finding herein the
refutation of Horatio Alger, Norman Vincent Peale, and other
"squares" whose philosophy can be very uncomfortable.

It lets them off the hook—the hook of *work,* effort, resilience, building, confrontation and, above all, *change.*

But I digress! I have grown serious too soon. Let's take a few
minutes and tiptoe through the terpsichorean tulips of Peter
twaddle. Some interviews follow which will lift the veil from certain
significant happenings in a hierarchical society. Ed Powerouse, administrative engineer at the Voltuppage Company, gave me his reaction to the book.

Yes, Mr. Batten, I was what you'd call a turned-on guy in under-
graduate school, and I vowed I'd become the best engineer in the
country. I suppose I was dumb, but I kept taking night school

[2] Laurence J. Peter and Raymond Hull, *The Peter Principle: Why Things Go Wrong,*
William Morrow & Co., Inc. (1970).

courses as the years went by, and I asked each boss how I could best use my full talents to contribute to the achievement of objectives. I was kind of hung up on the word *self-actualization*. I believed that the only guy I was competing with was me. And I tried hard to teach this to my kids. I really felt there was no limit to what I could accomplish in this country of ours, what with all the freedoms and opportunities we bump into every way we turn. I remember I had just turned forty-two when I picked up a copy of this book called *The Peter Principle* by Dr. Peter.

Well, Mr. Batten, I wised up quick when I read this book. If all I can look forward to is reaching my level of incompetence, I'd better begin to enjoy life more *now*. So I began to plan on making my job more secure and—I reasoned—why avoid that extra martini? You'll have to agree I had been pretty dumb. If I'm going to be obsolete anyway, why not enjoy the process?

Bill Guttey, production superintendent at the Fortitude Packing Company, told how he felt.

Look, Joe, I'll admit I've become a pretty good office politician. Yeah, I know you believe that performance is all that matters, but you've got to admit that it's a heck of a lot easier to use my seniority, my sheepskins, and some really skillful salesmanship to impress my boss than this performance bit. Believe it or not, there was a time when integrity was just about the most important word I knew. And then I had to come face to face with reality—the reality that everyone in the business world reaches his or her level of incompetence eventually. Well! Constantly practicing integrity can be wearing, and it's tough. This guy, Peter, has got to be right because he's a professor; he has a Ph.D.; and his book is a bestseller. How can you argue with a guy like that? He *knows!*

Is there an antidote? Is there a wellspring of pure, unsullied leadership substance which can wash away, burn off, or reduce to nothingness this "incompetence" dross?

Reflect for a moment, if you will, on a statement I have modestly termed "The Batten Principle":

> *The ultimate value of each individual is*
> *the sum of the values between his or her ears.*

Consider the case of the Lofty Pinnacle Dynamo Company. I received a call from Howard Piston, president. Mr. Piston was in a low mood.

"How," he asked wanly, "can I rejuvenate my team? Five of my vice presidents are convinced they have reached their levels of incompetence. Look at their track records. They were great until about six months ago when suddenly they got to talking about this incompetence bit." (I abhor executives who talk about "bits," but you can see what was happening to Mr. Piston.)

He showed me their records. What splendid performance records they had! Their names? Hy Grothe, vice president, sales; Elwood Charger, vice president, manufacturing; I. Cando, vice president, administration; Sam Stretchet, vice president, engineering.

"Mr. Piston," I said (soon I was calling him Howard), "the ultimate value of each individual is the sum of the values between his or her ears!"

He looked at me suspiciously. "Here now, Mr. Batten, what's all this? I thought you were an expert on tough-minded management."

"And so I am," I said, "but toughness does not mean hardness. Allow me to illustrate with two lists of traits, or values."

Hard-Minded Values (like granite)	*Tough-Minded Values* (like leather)
Activity-centered	Results-centered
Negative	Enthusiastic
Fragile	Durable
Rigid	Flexible
Grim	Cheerful
Arrogant	Poised yet warm
Go-getter	Go-giver
Expects the worst	Expects the best
Static	Hungry for personal growth
Fearful	Confident of future for company and self
Weak	Fibrous
Abrasive, blunt	Candid
Dwells on weaknesses	Builds on strengths
Pushes, drives	Leads
Expects little, dwells on weakness	Committed to talent actualization
Low expectations of self and others	High expectations of self and others

He still looked dubious. "Howard," I said, "each of your vice presidents is currently moving away from the tough-minded values toward the hard-minded values, and thus the total worth, productivity, or *value* of each is moving him toward the limbo known as obsolescence. Shun the twilight of "incompetence values," commit your organization to "excellence values" because the total worth of each of these managers is the sum of the values by which he or she lives, ergo, the values between his or her ears."

Howard's formerly dour visage was now aglow. "Ah!" he said. "this sounds great, but it also confuses me. Aren't these *behavioral principles?*"

"Yes," I said, puzzled. "Why?"

"Well, if you're really talking about *traits* or behavioral science principles, how can you, a management pragmatist, equate them with *tough-mindedness?*" Before I could answer, he exclaimed, "Now I see it! Management principles are nothing more nor less than behavioral science principles in action in a management context. You've been talking about applied *values* to produce organizational *value.*"

"Yes," I said, and again shared with him this thought:

> *The ultimate value of each person is the*
> *sum total of the values between his or her ears.*

Howard then wanted to know how soon a program of positive values could be presented to his "abominable no-men," and he was forthwith accommodated.

The results? The base canard known as the Peter Principle was banished to the provinces of the Lofty Pinnacle Dynamo Company's competitors and forward thrust was resumed. A Batten Breakthrough had happened!!

Tough-*minded* management is rooted in the conviction that the findings of behavioral *science*—skillfully blended with other interdisciplinary truths—enables one to approach an advanced state of the *art* of management. Please reflect on this at great length.

As I mused on this conversation with Howard, it came to me that perhaps the ultimate value of every *organization* is the sum of the values taught, thought, and wrought therein.

Glen Gaucherie, ecological and environmental consultant, was gloomy.

"Joe, it's no use. Pollution has gotten out of hand, and I fear for Earth's future."

"But, Glen," I reproached him, "where's that fiery zeal, that ardor for work, that motivational thrust for which you have become rightfully known? I've been confident of our ability to build a society of excellence because of people like *you.*"

"Yes," he sighed, "I *was* that way, and I'd like to be again, but Dr.

Peter in his diabolical books says ultimately *everything* goes *wrong*—and his credentials are impeccable. So what's the use?"

Here was the challenge! Here was the bland leading the bland when the situation cried out for zeal, ardor, courage, and skill. I obligingly presented him with The Batten Principle.

"But," Glen said, "this can be deadly, too, if you pursue and absorb incompetent values between the ears, you will only become more incompetent in practice!"

"Precisely," I snapped, "and, perhaps Dr. Peter is no villain after all. Perhaps he is only a seeker of truth and leaves the burden of refutation of his principle (?) up to each of us. Perhaps he hopes that each of us, Glen, will start with the person in the mirror and hurl *evidence* of excellence at that face."

Glen Gaucherie, no longer gloomy, was glowing. "I'll take the challenge," he grated, "I'll show him his 'principle' is only a theorem. Not for me, the path of the expedient, the gutless, the passive. For *me,* excelsior, tough-mindedness, growth, change, quest, and relevance. "Dr. Peter, beware!" I smiled.

I thought of the words of Niccolò Machiavelli in *The Prince:*

> There is nothing more difficult to take in hand, more perilous to
> conduct, or more uncertain in its success, than to take the lead in
> the introduction of a new order of things.

Let us begin.

Index

abilities and skills, in development, 35–36
accountability
 motivational climate and, 18
 in organizing for results, 56–57
accounting, profitability, 57–59
achievement, synergistic, 29
actualization, organizational, 209–212
Adler, Mortimer J., on will to lead, 212–213
Air Force planning procedure, 44–45
allies, resurgent, and management statesman, 158–159
analysis, in methods improvement, 28
Appley, Lawrence A., on management, 5
assignments
 clear-cut, in organizing for results, 54–55
 of strengths, 205–206
atmosphere
 clean-desk executive and, 130–131
 martinet and, 131–132

attitude
 drudgery and, 129–130
 leadership and, 7–8
authority, in organizing for results, 56–57
automation, as servant or master, 138–140

Batten Principle, 214
Batten's law of communication, 67
becoming
 courage and, 125
 in response to expectations, 198–199
beliefs, and development, 35
Black, James Menzies, 132
board of directors, and performance, 30–31
bossism, new styles in, 119–120
Bosted, John C., on free enterprise, 163
Bullis, Harry A., on free enterprise, 149–150, 151

219

business
  growth of conscience in, 164–165
  people in, 114–115

candor
  committees and, 110–111
  constructive innovation and, 115–116
  in counsel, 111–112
  as essential lubricant, 108–109
  face to face, 109–110
  politics and, 112–113
  practicality of, 116–117
  pull vs. push and, 120–121
  yes men and, 113
Carnegie, Andrew, on organization, 33
change, overcoming resistance to, 93–94
clean-desk executive, 130–131
committees, and candor, 110–111
Common Market, 159–160
communication
  Batten's law of, 67
  interviewing, 97–98
  memoranda, 97
  motivation and, 63–66
  in overcoming resistance to change, 93–94
  reports, 95–97
  selling with words, 98–100
  simplicity in, 94–95
  word picture in, 100
community, impact of integrity, 169–170
compensation, as defense mechanism, 86
compensation, executive, and development, 37
competitors, relations with, 157–158
conscience, business, growth of, 164–165
consistency, in planning, 45–46
consumers, relations with, 157
control
  categories, 74–76

defined, 73
  discipline and, 76–77
  feedback and, 78
  follow-up and, 80–81
  performance measurement and, 78–80
  self-supporting, 81–82
  of strengths, 208
costs of controls, 81–82
counsel vs. advice, 111
courage
  becoming and, 125
  course of least resistance and, 121–123
  imagination and, 123
  new styles in bossism and, 119–120
  problem solving in motivational climate and, 123–124
creativity and development, 38
Critique of Pure Reason (Kant), 190
cynicism, 87

daydreaming, as defense mechanism, 86
decision making
  integrity in, 168–169
  motivation and, 69–70
defense mechanisms, 86–87
delegating, in organizing for results, 55–56
development
  organization and, 33–34
  personal growth and, 39–40
  self-esteem and, 40
  separating pros from amateurs and, 37–39
  stretching and, 34–37
  structured approach, 33
  vs. training, 32
Dewey, John, on change, 193
dignity, 105
  concepts of, 3–4
discipline
  control and, 76–77
  executive and, 160

Dively, George S., on creative management, 71–72
Drucker, Peter, 43, 93
  on board of directors, 30
  on enterprise and plant community, 169
drudgery and attitude, 129–130

ease, pursuit of, 5–6
education of future, 188–189
electronic age
  automation as servant or master and, 138–140
  kaleidoscopic decade, 138
  mathematical parameters, 143–145
  objective view of, 140–142
  operations research and, 142–143
  organizational impact, 145–146
Emerson, Ralph Waldo, 183
emotion, motivation and, 70–72
empathy
  motivation and, 67–68
  warmth and, 135–136
employees, relations with, 157
evaluation, in methods improvement, 28–29
execution, in methods improvement, 29
executive
  clean-desk, 130–131
  delegating, 55–56
  disciplined, 160
  health of, 126–127
  as individual, 172–173
  isolation, imagination and, 10–11
  as member of society, 174–175
expectations
  becoming and, 198–199
  synergy and, 206–207

fear, 88–89
feedback and control, 78
follow-up and control, 80–81
force and development, 38
free enterprise
  for all, 161–163
  ideas that build and strengthen and, 148–150
  integrity and, 163–164
  sterility of materialism and, 150–151
  talk about profit and, 153–154
freewheeling, 90–92
Fromm, Erich
  on boredom, 188
  on passion for consumption, 192
future
  challenge to management, 177–185
  education, 188–189
  genetic engineering, 192–193
  labor, 187–188
  life span, 192
  medicine, 193
  mental abilities, 189–192
  minorities in, 212
  new person, 185–187
  new worlds to conquer, 193–194
  nuclear energy, 193
  population, 186–187
  tools, 195
  will to manage in, 212–217

Gallagher, James D., 146n
Gellerman, Saul W., on maximizing achievement potential, 84
genetic engineering, in the future, 192–193
Gibran, Kahlil, on work, 5
goals and needs in motivation, 61–63
government, relations with, 157
Guest, L. C., Jr., on managing data processing, 145–146

Hayakawa, S. I., 101
health
  as elementary common sense, 127–128
  executive, 126–127
  prescription for longevity and, 128–129

Henry, Edwin, on effective managers, 179–180
Herzberg, Frederick, 197
Hitler, Adolf, 189

imagination
  courage and, 123
  executive isolation and, 10–11
indecision, results of, 24–25
inhibitions, overcoming, 90–92
innovation, constructive, 115–116
integrity
  community impact of, 169–170
  defined, 163
  growth of business conscience and, 164–165
  naturalness of, 165–166
  old smoothie and, 167–168
  pervasive, 163–164
  young sophisticate and, 166–167
interests, in development, 36
interviewing, effective, 97–98
isolation, executive, and imagination, 10–11

Johnson, Wendell, on value of words, 94

Kant, Immanuel, 190

labor, in the future, 187–188
leadership
  motivation techniques, 62–63
  planning and, 46–47
  positive, 7–8
  qualities of, 46–47
  vacillating vice president, 46
life span, in the future, 192
Lincoln, James, 85
Lindbergh, Anne Morrow, on insincerity, 117
Long, George I., Jr., on motivational climate, 18
longevity, prescription for, 128–129

Machiavelli, Niccolò, on introducing new order of things, 217
management
  challenge of future, 177–185
  integrity in decision, 168–169
  mistakes within reason in, 9–10
  motivational climate and, 16–20
  need for purpose in, 6–7
  nice-guy, and performance, 27
  opportunity, 4–5
  self-knowledge in, 8–9
  stuff of, 132–133
management by objectives (MBO)
  assignment of strengths, 205–206
  control of strengths, 208
  development of strengths, 205
  human element and, 199–200
  need for significance and, 197–198
  organizational actualization and, 209–212
  strengths classification, 201–205
  strengths identification, 200–201
  strengths measurement, 207–208
  synergy and expectations, 206–207
management statesman
  as disciplined executive, 160
  Common Market and, 159–160
  obligations of, 155–158
  resurgent allies and, 158–159
manager
  as individual, 171–173
  motivation role, 66–68
  profile, 175–176
  in society, 174–175
The Man in Management (Steckle), 83
Marrow, Alfred J., on bored employee, 127–128
martinet, 131–132
Maslow, Abraham, 188, 197
materialism, sterility of, 150–151
Maytag Co., 10
MBO, *see* management by objectives
measurement
  of performance, 78–80
  of strengths, 207–208
medicine of future, 193

memoranda, 97
mental abilities of future, 189–192
methods improvement and performance, 27–29
mistakes, reasonable, 9–10
motivation
  common denominator in, 68–69
  communication and, 63–66
  decision making and, 69–70
  emotion and, 70–72
  manager's role in, 66–68
  needs and personal goals in, 61–63
motivational climate
  do's and don'ts, 14–15
  global goals and, 149
  mistakes within reason and, 10
  problem solving in, 123–124
  steps in achieving, 13–14
  taut ship and, 20–21
  top management and, 16–20

needs
  goals in motivation and, 61–63
  hierarchy of, 197, 198
nuclear energy of future, 193
Nunlist, Frank, on realizing potential, 190–192

operations research, techniques of, 142–143
opportunity, yesterday and today, 4–5
organization
  development and, 33–34
  organization development vs. organizational actualization and, 209–212
  will to manage and, 212–217
The Organization Man (Whyte), 1
organizing for results
  accountability in, 56–57
  clear-cut assignments in, 54–55
  delegating in, 55–56
  elements in, 49–50
  getting operational and, 50–52
  profitability accounting in, 57–59

teamwork in, 53–54
using talents in, 52–53
Otto, Herbert, 189

people
  in business, 114–115
  of future, 185–187
  "little," characteristics of, 84–86
  organization and, 211–212
performance
  dangers of realism and, 23–24
  making things happen, 25–27
  measurement and control, 78–80
  methods improvement and, 27–29
  nice-guy management and, 27
  return on investment and, 29–30
  salary and, 24–25
The Peter Principle (Peter and Hull), 213
philosophy and organization, 210
phony, defined, 102–104
physical attributes and development, 35
planning
  blueprint for, 44–45
  consistency in, 45–46
  leadership qualities and, 46–47
  for participation and cooperation, 42–44
  vacillating vice president and, 46
policies, and organization, 210
population of future, 186–187
positives, stressing, 83–84
Powell, J. Lewis, 70n
The Practice of Management (Drucker), 93
The Prince (Machiavelli), 217
problem solving, in motivational climate, 123–124
procedures and organization, 211
processes and organization, 211
procrastination, results of, 24–25
profit, talk about, 153–154
profitability accounting, 57–59
programs and organization, 211

projection, as defense mechanism, 86
purpose, need for, 6–7

Randall, Clarence B., on retirement, 134–135
rationalization, as defense mechanism, 86
Rensselaer Review, 193
reports, 95–97
responsibility, in organizing for results, 56
retirement, 134–135
return on investment, and performance, 29–30

salary and performance, 24–25
sarcasm, 87
Sears, Roebuck & Co., 124
security, search for, 2–3
self, knowledge of, 8–9
self-discipline and control, 77
self-esteem and development, 40
selling, better job of, 151–153
Shapley, Harlow, 194
Shepard, William P., on executive health, 126–127
skills and abilities, in development, 35–36
slackness, price of, 104–105
society
managers as members of, 174–175
weak spots, 148
Solzhenitsyn, Alexander, 107
Staley, John D., on cost-minded manager, 29
Stare, Frederick J., on heart trouble, 192
Steckle, Lynde, 83
stockholders, relations with, 156
strengths
assignment of, 205–206
classification of, 201–205
control of, 208
development and, 40, 205

identification of, 200–201
measurement of, 207–208
stretching, development and, 34–37, 38
synergy and expectations, 206–207

talent, wasted, and organizing for results, 52–53
teamwork, organizing and, 49, 53–54
tension, making asset of, 89–90
Terkel, Studs, 210
Terry, George R., on procedure, 96
tomorrow-mindedness, 124
training vs. development, 32
traits for leading real lives, 107

Uris, Auren, concept of tomorrow-mindedness, 124

values and development, 35
vice president, vacillating, 46
vision and development, 37–38
vitality, meaning of, 1–2
von Braun, Wernher, 6

warmth
and clean-desk executive, 130–131
and empathy, 135–136
Weiss, E. B., on extraterrestrial life, 194
White, Paul Dudley, 128
Whyte, William H., Jr., 1, 85
wisdom
as stuff of management, 132–133
as system of values, 133–134
words
selling with, 98–100
value of, 94
work, as life, 134–135
Working (Terkel), 210
Worthy, James C., on free enterprise, 162

yes men, and candor, 113–114
Yunich, David L., 99n

AMACOM Paperbacks

John Fenton	The A To Z Of Sales Management	$ 7.95	07580
Hank Seiden	Advertising Pure And Simple	$ 7.95	07510
Alice G. Sargent	The Androgynous Manager	$ 8.95	07601
John D. Arnold	The Art Of Decision Making	$ 6.95	07537
Oxenfeldt & Miller & Dickinson	A Basic Approach To Executive Decision Making	$ 7.95	07551
Curtis W. Symonds	Basic Financial Management	$ 7.95	07563
William R. Osgood	Basics Of Successful Business Planning	$ 7.95	07579
Dickens & Dickens	The Black Manager	$10.95	07564
Ken Cooper	Bodybusiness	$ 5.95	07545
Jones & Trentin	Budgeting	$12.95	07528
Laura Brill	Business Writing Quick And Easy	$ 5.95	07598
Rinella & Robbins	Career Power	$ 7.95	07586
Andrew H. Souerwine	Career Strategies	$ 7.95	07535
Beverly A. Potter	Changing Performance On The Job	$ 9.95	07613
Donna N. Douglass	Choice And Compromise	$ 8.95	07604
Philip R. Lund	Compelling Selling	$ 8.95	07506
Joseph M. Vles	Computer Basics	$ 6.95	07599
Hart & Schleicher	A Conference And Workshop Planner's Manual	$15.95	07003
Leon Wortman	A Deskbook Of Business Management	$14.95	07571
John D. Drake	Effective Interviewing	$ 8.95	07600
James J. Cribbin	Effective Managerial Leadership	$ 6.95	07504
Eugene J. Benge	Elements Of Modern Management	$ 5.95	07519
James E. Kristy & Susan Z. Diamond	Finance Without Fear	$10.95	07587
Edward N. Rausch	Financial Management For Small Business	$ 7.95	07585
Loren B. Belker	The First-Time Manager	$ 6.95	07588
Whitsett & Yorks	From Management Theory to Business Sense	$17.95	07610
Ronald D. Brown	From Selling To Managing	$ 7.95	07500
Murray L. Weidenbaum	The Future Of Business Regulation	$ 5.95	07533
Craig S. Rice	Getting Good People And Keeping Them	$ 8.95	07614
Charles Hughes	Goal Setting	$ 4.95	07520
Richard E. Byrd	A Guide To Personal Risk Taking	$ 7.95	07505
Charles Margerison	How To Assess Your Managerial Style	$ 6.95	07584
S.H. Simmons	How To Be The Life Of The Podium	$ 8.95	07565
D. German & J. German	How To Find A Job When Jobs Are Hard To Find	$ 7.95	07592

W.H. Krause	How To Get Started As A Manufacturer's Representative	$ 8.95	07574
Sal T. Massimino	The Complete Book of Closing Sales	$ 5.95	07593
William A. Delaney	How To Run A Growing Company	$ 6.95	07590
Dean B. Peskin	A Job Loss Survival Manual	$ 5.95	07543
H. Lee Rust	Jobsearch	$ 7.95	07557
Marc J. Lane	Legal Handbook For Small Business	$ 7.95	07612
George T. Vardaman	Making Successful Presentations	$10.95	07616
Norman L. Enger	Management Standards For Developing Information Systems	$ 5.95	07527
Ray A. Killian	Managing Human Resources	$ 6.95	07556
Elam & Paley	Marketing For The Non-Marketing Executive	$ 5.95	07562
Edward S. McKay	The Marketing Mystique	$ 6.95	07522
Donald E. Miller	The Meaningful Interpretation Of Financial Statements	$ 6.95	07513
Robert L. Montgomery	Memory Made Easy	$ 5.95	07548
Donald P. Kenney	Minicomputers	$ 7.95	07560
Frederick D. Buggie	New Product Development Strategies	$ 8.95	07602
Dale D. McConkey	No-Nonsense Delegation	$ 4.95	07517
Hilton & Knoblauch	On Television	$ 6.95	07581
Ellis & Pekar	Planning Basics For Managers	$ 6.95	07591
Alfred R. Oxenfeldt	Pricing Strategies	$10.95	07572
Blake & Mouton	Productivity: The Human Side	$ 5.95	07583
Daniels & Barron	The Professional Secretary	$ 7.95	07576
Herman R. Holtz	Profit From Your Money-Making Ideas	$ 8.95	07553
William E. Rothschild	Putting It All Together	$ 7.95	07555
J.F. Engelberger	Robotics In Practice	$24.95	07587
Don Sheehan	Shut Up And Sell!	$ 7.95	07615
Roger W. Seng	The Skills Of Selling	$ 7.95	07547
Hannan & Berrian & Cribbin & Donis	Success Strategies For The New Sales Manager	$ 8.95	07566
Paula I. Robbins	Successful Midlife Career Change	$ 7.95	07536
Leon Wortman	Successful Small Business Management	$ 8.95	07503
D. Bennett	TA And The Manager	$ 4.95	07511
George A. Brakeley, Jr.	Tested Ways To Successful Fund-Raising	$ 8.95	07568
William A. Delaney	Tricks Of The Manager's Trade	$ 6.95	07603
Alec Benn	The 27 Most Common Mistakes In Advertising	$ 8.95	07554
James Gray, Jr.	The Winning Image	$ 6.95	07611
John Applegath	Working Free	$ 6.95	07582
Allen Weiss	Write What You Mean	$ 5.95	07544
Richard J. Dunsing	You And I Have Simply Got To Stop Meeting This Way	$ 5.95	07558